Relocating

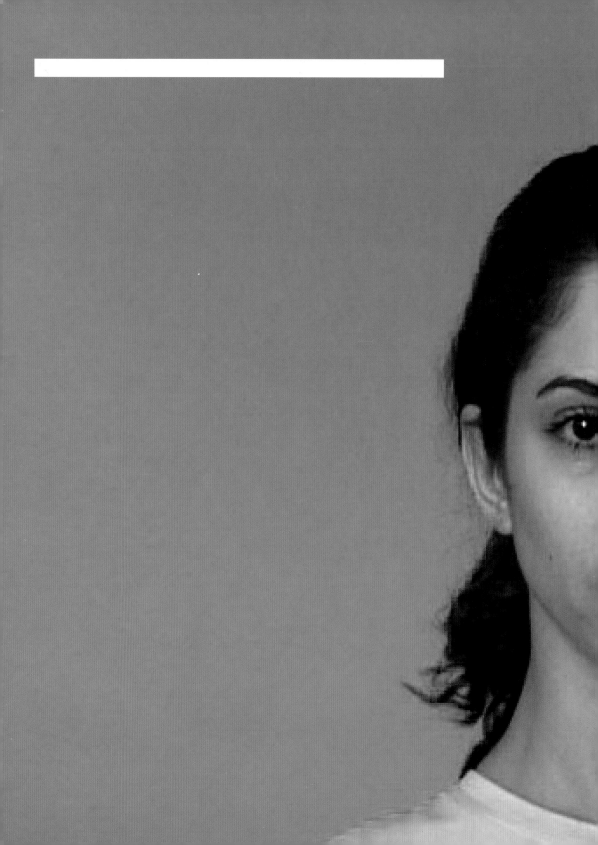

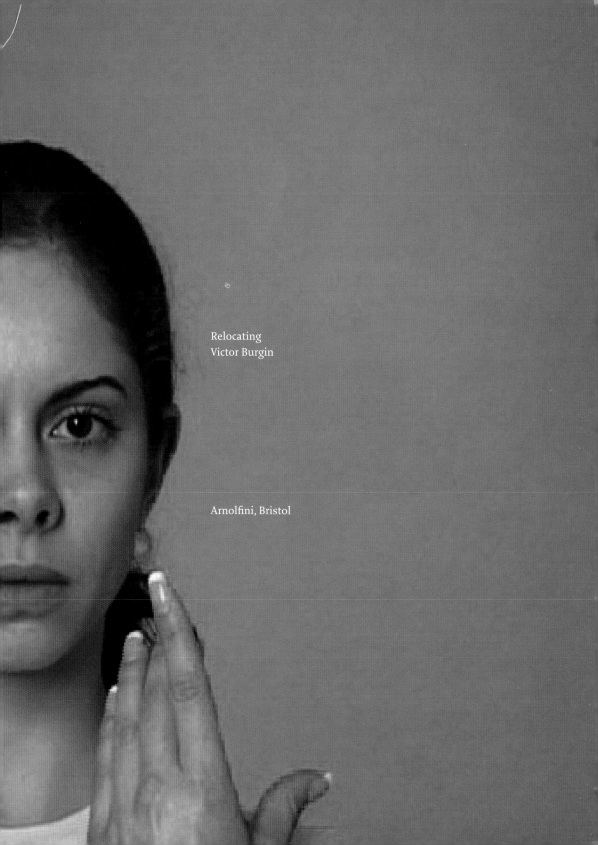

Relocating
Victor Burgin

Arnolfini, Bristol

Arnolfini
16 Narrow Quay
Bristol BS1 4QA, UK
www.arnolfini.demon.co.uk
Director: Caroline Collier
Senior Curator: Catsou Roberts

Design: Lucy or Robert, or@either.co.uk

Production: Print Select
Distributor: Cornerhouse

Arnolfini wish to thank Nick Barley, Kathy Rae Huffman, Lynda Morris, Robin Klassnik, Lucy Steeds

This book is published on the occasion of the exhibition *Listen to Britain: Works by Victor Burgin*, curated by Catsou Roberts, Senior Curator at Arnolfini, Bristol. A companion volume rather than a catalogue, the book includes artworks not featured in the exhibition.

Exhibitions:
Listen to Britain: Works by Victor Burgin
21 September – 17 November 2002
Arnolfini, Bristol

Listen to Britain: Works by Victor Burgin
11 January – 23 February 2003
Cornerhouse, Manchester

Listen to Britain
15 January – 22 February 2003
Norwich Gallery, Norwich

Watergate
9 October – 1 December 2002
Matt's Gallery, London

Front cover: *Listen to Britain*, 2002, detail
Back cover: *Venise*, 1993, detail

The visitor from the north imagines that Rome will supplement his own existence and supply what he lacks: it only gradually dawns on him, to his great discomfort, that he has to alter his reactions completely and start from the very beginning.

Goethe, *Italian Journey*

*One has to write as one lives, first for one's own sake, and then
for the sake of a few congenial souls.*

Goethe, *Italian Journey*

Preface

This book is published on the occasion of Arnolfini's monographic exhibition of Victor Burgin's work. The book, like the exhibition, is timed to coincide with Victor Burgin's recent return to Britain after thirteen years in the United States, and both are intended to provide an overview of his work, as well as offer insight into various aspects of his practice since the late 1960s, when he emerged as one of the most important proponents of conceptual art.

In addition to his work as an artist, Burgin is a well-known and widely published academic, and is celebrated as an important theorist and teacher. He returned to London in the autumn of 2001 to take up the position of Millard Professor of Fine Art at Goldsmiths College, University of London.

Victor Burgin's work has engendered critical debate about issues of photography and the moving image, and through its originality and experimentation across a variety of media – including new technologies such as digital video – Burgin's work continues to make an important contribution to contemporary artistic practice.

Caroline Collier
Director, Arnolfini

Preceding pages: studies for *Orfeo*, 2002.
Work in progress for the London Symphony Orchestra.

Some introductory information leading to the possible location of Victor Burgin

Catsou Roberts

In 1965, as a recent graduate from the Painting School of London's Royal College of Art, Victor Burgin left Great Britain to relocate to the United States for the first time. There, in the 'hothouse atmosphere'[1] that was the School of Art and Architecture at Yale in the mid-1960s, he was taught by Donald Judd, Robert Morris, Ad Reinhardt, Frank Stella and Helen Frankenthaler, among other artists who commanded attention in the New York art scene of the time. Despite a modernist training at Yale, Burgin began to entertain the idea of a complete rupture with modernism and Greenbergian notions of art. Introduced to minimalism and an assortment of philosophical texts,[2] his practice evolved beyond formalist priorities and developed along the lines of what would eventually be termed 'conceptual art'.

1. Tony Godfrey, 'Sex, Text, Politics: An Interview with Victor Burgin', *Block*, issue 7, 1982, p. 3.

2. Burgin received his first training in philosophy from Iris Murdoch at the Royal College of Art. He later studied philosophy as his 'academic elective' in the School of Art and Architecture at Yale.

On his return to England in 1967, Burgin began to produce a series of instructions, typed on index cards, for the realisation of potential artworks latent in the language on the cards. Within this compilation of ideas was the two-sentence description for making *Photopath*, a work that was to be reified as part of the groundbreaking exhibition *When Attitudes Become Form* of 1969. *Photopath*, a series of photographs of a path along the floor over which the images were then superimposed, was intended as a solution to the historic 'here but not here' problem,[3] and the work remains a touchstone of ideationally based practice.[4] Burgin's essay 'Situational Aesthetics', published in the same year as *When Attitudes Become Form*, insisted that the artwork be posited in terms of 'situations' and psychological experiences rather than objects. This essay has also remained a critical document for the study of contemporary art.[5] After the inaugural *When Attitudes Become Form*, Burgin participated in many other historically significant international exhibitions that addressed the dematerialised and conceptual nature of contemporary practice, for example, *Konzept-Kunst, Idee und Material, Art as Thought Process, 557, 087, Information* and *Idea Structures*, in addition to exhibitions presenting the emergence of a particularly British strand of conceptual art – such as *Arte Inglese Oggi 1960-1976, The British Avant Garde, New English Inquiry* and *Un Certain Art Anglais* – and more general international shows such as *Documenta 5* and the *36th Venice Biennial*.

By 1970, Burgin was internationally recognised as a pioneer of conceptual art. As it became increasingly obvious that the term 'conceptualism' failed to designate a coherent artistic approach, Burgin emerged as one of the most forceful and singular voices in the ensuing debates between its various practitioners. Like others of his contemporaries resistant to the commercialism of the art market, and aware of the newly emerging environmentalist issues, Burgin balked at the aimless accumulation of material art objects. He understood that art need not necessarily add more physical materials to the world, but could take the form of an intervention within the existing fabric of material things. His work *Room* for the *Idea Structures* show at Camden Arts Centre in London featured a large and apparently empty room. Pasted to the blank white walls were eighteen pieces of paper, each containing a typewritten phrase. Composed in a 'performative' mode of address – for example, 'All substantial things which constitute this room' – these propositions drew the viewer's attention to the very act of seeing, and highlighted the role of memory in perception.[6] The 'physical' aspect of the artwork consisted merely of a few strips of paper, but it succeeded in incorporating the existing

3. Godfrey, op. cit., p. 4.

4. For a fuller discussion of this, and many of the subsequent works mentioned, see texts by Stephen Bann, Peter Osborne and Françoise Parfait below.

5. Originally published in *Studio International*, vol. 178, no. 915, October 1969, pp. 118-21. See Stephen Bann's text below for a fuller discussion.

6. Godfrey, op. cit., p. 5.

7. *The New Art*, London: Hayward Gallery, Arts Council of Great Britain, 1972; reprinted in *Victor Burgin*, Barcelona: Fundació Antoni Tàpies, 2001, p. 85.

8. Victor Burgin, *Between*, Oxford: Blackwell, 1986, p. 12.

9. Godfrey, op. cit., pp. 9-10.

10. Burgin would return to the guerrilla poster format in 1989 in Minneapolis with a poster version of *Minnesota Abstract*.

architectural structure, and in radically transforming the viewer's experience of the entire gallery space.

Burgin's philosophical position *vis-à-vis* the role of art and its physical context led him to consider the larger arena of everyday life and its political dimensions – consequently, his work started to incorporate elements of Marxist thought. He began 'looking into art's *instrumentality* in a wider social context'[7] as he attempted to 'deconstruct the ideological divisions between the inside and the outside of the gallery'.[8] Photography became his principal medium and, paired with text, his work delivered a hard-hitting criticism of capitalism and hegemonic power through a photo-text style appropriated from advertising. Burgin's use of quotidian systems of signification – writing and photography (what Burgin called a 'scripto-visual discourse') – was a response to the 'dynamics of the social world about [him]'.[9] *Possession*, from 1976, took the form of five hundred posters pasted around Newcastle's city centre.[10] The poster shows a chic couple embracing, accompanied by the question: 'What does possession mean to you?'. Below the seductive image the statistic, '7% of our population own 84% of our wealth', shakes off any romantic reverie elicited by the glamorous photograph.

Possession
1976, 109 x 84 cm, 500 copies
posted in the centre of
Newcastle-upon-Tyne

The emphasis on text and narrative structure in Burgin's work prompted his early interest in semiotics and post-structuralism. The work of Roland Barthes, with its analysis of the rhetorical strategies of imagery and modes of connotative communication, was of particular importance to Burgin, and writing theory became a fundamental component of his own practice. By the mid-1970s, the artist was regularly contributing articles to journals and magazines on a range of cultural issues including semiotics, photography and modernism. Soon he was publishing books, and was to be acknowledged as one of the most influential critical theorists whose essays, noted for their clarity and cogent arguments, have been fundamental contributions to the literature of postmodernism. The success of Burgin's critical writing ran parallel with his artistic practice as he continued to exhibit widely and play a crucial role in the landscape of international contemporary art. His signature black-and-white photo-text works of the late 1970s, such as *UK 76*, *US 77* and *Zoo 78*, employed documentary 'street'-style photographic imagery, which he combined with texts in the manner of glossy magazines. These works exemplify the artist's frequent and increasing practice of referring to specific time/place co-ordinates. *UK 76* focused on class and social inequities in Britain, while *US 77* – made during Burgin's second relocation to the United States – moved away from the artist's 'residual economistic Marxism' to consider the construction of the subject in a patriarchal and media-dominated society.[11] The new series introduced a feminist discourse, and was less direct in its ideological message: it opened more subtle and ambiguous relationships between image and text. The work weaves together three distinct forms of language, or 'voices', and draws on what might metaphorically be termed the 'unconscious' of the image – the possible chains of associations that viewers might trace across and between individual sections. Burgin has referred to *US 77* as his 'road movie', a kind of 'static film' where the 'individual scenes have collapsed inwards upon themselves so that the narrative connections have become lost'.[12] With *Zoo 78*, structures of oppression in specular forms of surveillance became a key concern. Burgin addressed the power and function of the technical apparatus of photography itself, alluding to Foucauldian ideas of the panopticon. Having been through a period of producing work that represented various aspects of class politics, Burgin now became concerned with issues of gender politics and sexuality, which in turn led him to questions of unconscious fantasy.

By the early 1980s, Burgin's interest in psychoanalysis, implicit in earlier works in his references to Freud, had become explicit. *Tales from Freud*, a suite of five related photo-text works,[13] extended the ever-widening range of references within Burgin's artistic practice to include such themes as fetishism and voyeurism. In discussing *Olympia*, Burgin referred to the need, when viewing the work, to appeal to 'dream-logic' rather than 'common-sense'.[14] Its multi-level references to scopophilia, sexual identity, representation, psychoses, surveillance and patriarchal authority offer an 'endless spiral of interpretation'.[15] As with other works that present fragmentary clues drawn from literature, mythology, geographic and social history – in both image and narrative – *Olympia* sends the viewer darting restlessly between discrete panels of the work for meanings which cannot be 'consumed', but must be '*produced* in the active process of looking, reading, comparing, interpreting'.[16] The exhibition space thus enters the 'general arena of sites of contemporary

11. Burgin, op. cit., p. 40.

12. Ibid.

13. *In Lyon* (1980), *In Grenoble* (1981), *Gradiva* (1982), *Olympia* (1982), *Portia* (1983).

14. Letter from Victor Burgin to an undisclosed collector, printed in Burgin, op. cit., p. 137.

15. Ibid.

16. Ibid.

17. Ibid., p. 156.

18. Ibid., p. 154.

19. Elisabeth Lebovici, 'Burgin Entre Signe et Sens', *Libération*, 2 October, 1991, pp. 37-38.

experience . . . characterised not so much by the *image*, but rather by the continual *exchange* of one image for another'.[17] In this way, as with so much of Burgin's work, the piece extends beyond the immediate physical object to include the space between the panels, and the space of the motile viewer, creating an installational aspect around two-dimensional work.

With *In Lyon* and the closely related *In Grenoble*, Burgin began to engage with the specificity of particular cities – an abiding preoccupation in most of his subsequent work. Burgin has written about *In Lyon*: 'I see the work as a whole as a condensation of a complex of images/ideas centred around the imbrication of the psychic and the social, of sexuality and politics.' This could be said of many of his other works from that time and since. Cinema – in particular Hitchcock's – is another frame of reference that had entered Burgin's crowded repertoire by the 1980s, most explicitly in his 1984 work, *The Bridge*. The artist's aversion to conventional, linear narrative (he is a self-confessed 'diagephobe' who 'would probably literally suffocate if [he] were to be incarcerated in a theatre for the duration of a play')[18] engendered a critical relationship with narrative structure. *The Bridge* is a distillation of one of *Vertigo's* climactic scenes, and coalesces around a single moment in Hitchcock's film when the heroine, having jumped in despair into San Francisco Bay, is rescued by her obsessed admirer. The work draws on the memory of the film fiction (Burgin has said, 'I'm more interested in the film we remember than the one on the screen')[19] while the stylisation of the staged images – reflecting the artifice of cinema and theatre – signal a shift from Burgin's earlier 'documentary-style' photographs.

The figure of a drowning woman in *The Bridge* simultaneously refers to Hitchcock's heroine and to literary and art historical representations of the death of Ophelia. Burgin's dialogical relationship to the history of art, also evident in other earlier works – notably *In Grenoble* with its painting by Claude, or *Olympia* with Manet's eponymous painting – is foregrounded in *Office at Night*. Based on Edward Hopper's 1940s painting of the same name, this six-part piece also introduced colour into Burgin's work. Equally significant is the entrance of Isotypes (a system of pictograms developed in 1936 as an attempt at universal communication) which form a linguistic mode parallel to the written word, lassoing together the disparate spatial worlds of exterior and interior. The didactic, instructional tone of these iconographic messages – now pervasive with the widespread use of personal

19

computers – carry an oppressive sense of social and hierarchical order, reflecting the claustrophobic atmosphere of the conventional office environment where the work is staged (and recalling the setting of Burgin's *Performative/Narrative* of 1971). With works such as *Family Romance* the question of identity – another persistent concern for Burgin – is widened from gender and sexuality to encompass national and ethnic identity. Burgin's digital montage of images derived from the Hollywood classic *South Pacific* reconfigures traditional interpersonal power relationships by making manifest relations between characters that had remained only latent in the film.

In the early 1990s, after he had relocated to the United States for the third time in 1988, Burgin's work took a new and decisive direction with the use of video. His first video work, *Venise*, from 1993, is, like *Family Romance*, implicitly about identity as it considers exile, immigration, dislocation and alienation. Fundamentally, however, *Venise* is also about cities. *Venise* is, according to Burgin, a '"psycho-documentary" – (n)either fact (n)or fiction'.[20] The video features San Francisco and Marseilles, cities which each provide a backdrop for two related fictional works: Hitchcock's *Vertigo* and the novel by Pierre Boileau and Thomas Narcejac on which the film is based (which itself is derived from the myth of Orpheus and Eurydice). Burgin interweaves and overlaps these two parallel narratives – which are, in turn, stories about dualism and doubling – to form a dextrously structured work that mirrors and folds back onto itself.

Love Stories #2, an installation from 1996 using three monitors, exploits the elements of sound and movement, and their inverse – silence and fixity. Each monitor, set upon a slender plinth, shows a different loop of surveillance-type footage. Shot in public spaces in San Francisco and Las Vegas, these mundane scenarios of anonymous individuals are shown in slow motion – sometimes nearly grinding to a halt – thus imbuing their banal actions with a sense of melodrama. Burgin has said, 'I am particularly interested in the space between the still and the moving image, which is why there are passages in my works that call on the type of attention normally reserved for paintings. For example, at times the images may appear to be static although in fact they are not.'[21] The silent footage in this work periodically yields to screens of saturated colour accompanied by fragments of dialogue from classic Hollywood movie soundtracks. Each excerpt, spoken by a female protagonist, encapsulates her relationship to a significant other – resuming

Minnesota Abstract, 1989
Poster version, Minneapolis

20. *Victor Burgin*, Barcelona: Fundació Antoni Tàpies, 2001, p. 192.

Burgin's investigation of the psychosexual construction of the subject. The impeccably delivered lines are in stark contrast to the patently unstaged movements of the individuals captured on camera. It is the viewer's desire to forge a coherent narrative that initiates a cross-semination between these disparate elements. The narrative implications are further complicated by yet another element. Hovering above and uniting these three columnar elements, a single line of text stretches across the wall like a structural beam: 'Driving Fast on Empty Freeways'. The sentence, at odds with the laboured movements of the figures on the screen, evokes the American dream of the 'open road' and independent and unfettered mobility.

With *Some Cities*, published in 1996, the artist's exploration of particular cities through layers of political, cultural, historical and personal narratives, took the form of a book. The resonances between place and text in this work are a constant feature of Burgin's practice, and one that crystallises with the projected video pieces of the last decade. Each video was made in response to a specific exhibition commission, and usually take the host city – Budapest, Weimar, Paris, Washington or Barcelona, for example – as a point of departure. These works include *Szerelmes Levelek/Love Letters* (1997), *Lichtung* (1998-99), *Another Case History* (1999), *Nietzsche's Paris* (1999–2000), *Watergate* (2000), *Elective Affinities* (2000–01). Many of these include panoramas, the circling movement of the camera recalling the circling of the gallery in such early text works as *Room*, and in such 'total surround' photo/text installations as *US77*. Burgin has written, 'In everyday life the video image is associated mainly with television. The projected image is associated mainly with cinema. A large image on a gallery wall is associated with painting or photography. I think of my video works as situated in the space where associations to such specific institutions and practices overlap.'[22]

Burgin's single-screen video projection work *Watergate* was commissioned by the Corcoran Museum of Art, Washington, DC, and first shown in the context of the 2000–01 Corcoran Biennial. Burgin shot his material in the American Romantic Painting gallery of the museum, and in a Washington hotel room overlooking the Watergate apartment complex. The paintings in the gallery in effect summarise a nineteenth-century American cultural history, from the *Ruins of the Parthenon* to *The Last of the Buffalo*. A reproduction of one of the paintings, Frederic Church's *Niagara* (1857), hangs in the hotel room. In Burgin's video, a circling of the gallery first gives

21. Victor Burgin, 'Spring 2000 Robert Gwathmey Lectures', New York: Cooper Union for the Advancement of Science and Art, 2000, p. 44. reprinted in ibid., p. 189.

22. *Victor Burgin*, op. cit., p. 189.

21

way to a panorama of the hotel room, and then to a renewed tour of the gallery walls in a title sequence derived from the labels accompanying the paintings. A woman whose voice is heard over the images of the gallery reads an edited passage from Jean-Paul Sartre's *Being and Nothingness*, in which the philosopher asks what it means to say that we can 'see' that someone is not there. The title sequence is accompanied by an aria from one of Handel's Italian cantatas, in which the singer repeats a single sentence: *Alla salma infedel porga la pena* ('Inflict punishment on a faithless body'). Technically, as in his previous videos, Burgin constructs his work in a space between still and moving images. For this work, he began by making still images using a digital panoramic camera. He reworked these images on the computer, converting the stills to virtual reality movies in order to make the camera movements. The point of view given in the final video is therefore that of a virtual, rather than real, camera.

Elective Affinities, made in response to a commission from the Antoni Tàpies Foundation in Barcelona, features Mies van der Rohe's historic pavilion. Mies's famous building epitomises the modernist architectural integration of interior and exterior space; as Burgin has remarked, 'The space behaves like a Möbius strip'.[23] Burgin imagines a *temporal* integration within the pavilion – originally built in 1929 and reconstructed in 1986 – in which the building today comes to be 'haunted' by seven decades of Barcelona's history.[24] The sense of a recursive looping of time is reinforced by reference to Penelope – the faithful wife of the absent Odysseus – who unravelled by night her weaving of the day, starting her handiwork anew each morning to keep the future at bay.

23. Ibid., p. 252.

24. Ibid.

Throughout all the years of his practice Burgin's work has been consistently characterised by an austere and elegant formal restraint. Its visual impact derives from the compressed and telegraphic aspect of his images. These combine with his terse and lapidary textual components – written or aural – to generate a complex and intellectually dense whole that progressively unfolds the deeper the viewer reaches into its reservoir of references and associations (Burgin has said, 'all my work is about psychical space'). Burgin has always insisted on the active role of the viewer.

25. Victor Burgin, *Between*, Oxford: Blackwell, 1986, p. 138.

26. From a talk given to art students in 1983, printed in *Victor Burgin*, Barcelona: Fundació Antoni Tàpies, 2001, p. 163.

Against the tendency of art to become a passive 'spectator sport' he chooses to provide 'occasions for interpretation, rather than objects for consumption'.[25] For Burgin, 'art is a way of thinking', and he once thought of his work as contributing to a theoretical project. There are those who have hastily assumed that the key to Burgin's work is to be found in his theoretical writings, rather than in their own act of engagement with the work. Burgin has replied (he was speaking of *In Grenoble*, but the remark could be applied to his entire output): 'You *don't* need a knowledge of psychoanalytic theory to deal with work like this – you simply need to know how to dream.'[26]

UK 76
1976, three of eleven sections,
each 100 x 150 cm.

Love Stories # 2 video installation, 1996

DRIVING   FAST

O N   E M P T Y   F R E E W A Y S

DRIVING FAST

ON EMPTY FREEWAYS

DRIVING FAST

ON   EMPTY   FREEWAYS

DRIVING   FAST

ON   EMPTY   FREEWAYS

John Stahl
Leave Her to Heaven
soundtrack fragment, Gene Tierney

DRIVING FAST

ON EMPTY FREEWAYS

Alfred Hitchcock
Vertigo
soundtrack fragment, Kim Novak

DRIVING   FAST

Albert Lewin
Pandora and the Flying Dutchman
soundtrack fragment, Ava Gardner

ON   EMPTY   FREEWAYS

Watergate video projection, 2000

George Frideric Handel
Cantata
La Lucrezia
Aria: 'Alla salma infedel porga la pena', Magdalena Kožená

I have an appointment with Peter at four o'clock.

I arrive at the café a quarter of an hour late. Peter is always on time. Will he have waited for me?

I look at the room and I say, 'He is not here.'

Is there an intuition of the absence of Peter, or does the negation come only with judgement?

At first sight it seems absurd to speak of intuition here, since there cannot be an intuition of nothing, and since the absence of Peter is precisely this nothing.

Everyday language, however, bears witness to this intuition. Do we not say, for example, 'I saw right away that he was not there'?

It is certain that the café itself is a fullness of being – with its tables, its booths, its mirrors, its light, its smoky atmosphere, and the sounds of voices, rattling saucers and footsteps that fill it. And all the intuitions of detail I can have are filled by these odors, these sounds, these colors. Similarly, the actual presence of Peter in a place I do not know is also a fullness of being.

It seems that we find fullness everywhere. But we must observe that, in perception, there is always the construction of a figure on a ground. No object, no group of objects, is especially suited to be organized as either ground or figure: it all depends on the direction of my attention. When I enter this café, to look for Peter, all the objects in the café are synthetically organized as the ground against which Peter is given as having to appear. And this organization of the café as ground is a first nihilation. Each element of the room – person, table, chair – tries to isolate itself, to lift itself upon the ground constituted by the totality of other objects, only to fall back again into the indifferentiation of this ground, to be diluted in this ground. For the ground is that which is seen only as superfluous, as the object of a purely marginal attention.

So this first nihilation of all the figures, which appear and are swallowed up in the total equivalence of a ground, is the necessary condition for the appearance of the principal figure, which is here the person of Peter. And this nihilation is given to my intuition, I am witness to the successive fading of all the objects that I look at – especially the faces, which detain me for an instant ('Could that be Peter?') but which as quickly go out of focus precisely because they 'are not' the face of Peter. If, nevertheless, I should at last discover Peter, my intuition would be filled by a solid element, I would be suddenly fascinated by his face and all the café would organize itself around him.

But Peter is not here.

This does not mean that I discover his absence in some precise place in the establishment. For Peter is absent from all of the café. His absence freezes the café in its fading. The café remains ground, it persists in offering itself as an undifferentiated totality to my only marginal attention, it slides in the background, it pursues its nihilation.

But it only makes itself ground for a determinate figure, a figure it carries everywhere in front of it, that it presents to me everywhere; and this figure, which slips constantly between my look and the solid and real objects of the café, is precisely a perpetual fading; it is Peter raising himself as nothingness against the ground of nihilation of the café.

So that what is offered to the intuition is a fluttering of nothingness: the nothingness of the ground, the nihilation of which summons and demands the appearance of the figure, and that of the figure – nothingness which slides as a nothing on the surface of the ground.

This is what serves as foundation for the judgement . . .

'Peter is not here.'

Ruins of the Parthenon
1880
Sanford Robinson Gifford
American

View of Marshfield
1865–70
Martin Johnson Heade
American

Tamaca Palms
1854
Frederic Edwin Church
American

The Greek Slave
1846
Hiram Powers
American

Mount Corcoran
1876–77
Albert Bierstadt
American

Niagara
1857
Frederic Edwin Church
American

The Last of the Buffalo
1888
Albert Bierstadt
American

The Sun Vow
1905
Hermon A. MacNeil
American

Lacrosse Playing among the Sioux Indians
1851
Seth Eastman
American

The Departure
1837
Thomas Cole
American

The Return
1837
Thomas Cole
American

Endymion
1874
William Rinehart
American

Victor Burgin's Critical Topography

Stephen Bann

'What job does the artist do that is fundamentally different from the jobs done by his contemporaries in other fields?' asked Victor Burgin of his readers in his 1973 book-work entitled *Work and Commentary*. He immediately rules out a reply along the lines: 'Artists make things which please the eye.' This, as he rightly asserts, is a feature that would apply to many other fields of activity. He has, however, an answer ready to hand that will not fall under this objection. It is an answer, he claims, that will be 'retrospectively applicable to works from all historical periods and therefore resistant to passing fashion in argument'. The artist's job involves 'consideration of the codes we use to communicate with one another', and thus the 'sieves' processing the facts 'from which we construct our pictures of the world'. Burgin's way of characterising it is as follows:

A job for the artist which no one else does is to dismantle existing communication codes and to recombine some of their elements into structures which can be used to generate new pictures of the world. This definition of an art activity allows for the use of all codes across the entire range of the technologies by which they are expressed. Some, but not all, painting and sculpture is therefore incorporated within this definition. Nevertheless, committing a fundamental category error, most of the art community continue to treat work which has been 'differentially' determined in terms of the historically orientated discourse which originally evolved around painting and sculpture.

The argument is clear so far. It is not a question of separating off the art of the past, let alone of excluding from the scope of his decision traditional media and practices like painting and sculpture. The point is that past art has continued to be evaluated in terms of the categories used to define and describe it at the point of its production. Much of it may indeed have been assessed in terms of the degree to which it 'pleased the eye'. If we reorientate ourselves along the lines which Burgin recommends, we can recognise that the dismantling and recombination of codes to 'generate pictures of the world' is a criterion that applies to art throughout the ages – or at least to the art that genuinely matters. Burgin goes on to suggest that this attitude should also result in a different way of looking at the work of particular contemporary artists. It should no longer be a matter of considering how 'conceptual artist X' relates to LeWitt or Duchamp:

We would be concerned rather with what we might say about it in terms of such disparate entities as commercial cinema or extant moral and political beliefs. If our attention were directed on the artist's work alone, the work would not be viewed as a succession of stages in his professional evolution. It would be analysed in terms of underlying themes and formal motifs which, although undergoing transformations, are always present in what he does. This is not to say that the historical dimension is to be ignored but merely that it should no longer be allowed to dominate.

I have allowed myself these rather long quotations from a text written about thirty years ago because they still seem to define admirably the challenge that Burgin's art embodies. In the 1970s, much of the material that he was exhibiting consisted of large framed photographic sequences, involving printed commentary either juxtaposed or superimposed on the image itself. In 1995, however, the recent work that he chose to illustrate in the *Edge of Town* catalogue was a 'permanent video installation for the Ville d'Orléans'.[1] Yet this progressive exploitation of new technologies appears in itself fairly uninteresting compared with the remarkable consistency of the underlying themes and propositions in his work.

I want to use the present text as an opportunity to look back at some of the claims implied in Burgin's statement of 1973: 'What job does the artist do . . . ?' There is certainly no less of a need to ask that question now, after successive waves of fashion have peaked and receded, than there was in the early 1970s when the onset

1. *The Edge of Town*, box/catalogue, Hartford: Joseloff Gallery, 1995. Burgin describes the work as 'a large video projection screen suspended at the place of transit between the "high tech" and "no tech" floors of the building'.

of minimalism and conceptualism appeared to be turning the traditional aesthetic criteria on their head.

About one point, it is possible to agree straight away without much fear of objection. Where Burgin implies that the history of art itself must be saved from historicism, he can direct us to the intervening course of events for his justification. Indeed, he himself not much later contributed to the little collection of essays, *The New Art History*, which signalled the widespread renewal of art-historical method along the lines which he had predicted.[2] Art historians may not talk so much nowadays about 'codes' and 'structures', and the special pertinence of those particular analytic terms to the period in which Burgin was initially writing need not be emphasised. But the legacy of the 'New Art History' of the 1980s has been the debate over 'visual culture' in the past decade. Clearly there are many art historians who give the privilege in their work to tracing the diachronic evolution of 'painting and sculpture', and there are worthwhile reasons for doing so. But few of them have remained unaffected by the repositioning of art history to encompass the wider cultural objective of studying the way in which images generate 'new pictures of the world'.

Still, there can be little danger of confusing the artist's job with that of the art historian. The same may not be so clearly the case with the relationship between the artist's role that Burgin advocates, and the more amorphous role of the 'cultural critic'. Here it may well be helpful to begin by studying the interesting convergence between Burgin's commitment and a distinctive type of cultural commentary that was developing in the period following the end of the Second World War, and implied a certain similarity of approach. For example, I have often explained aspects of the study of 'visual culture' by juxtaposing the material that Marshall McLuhan gathered together in the immediate post-war period for his remarkable study *The Mechanical Bride*, with the images and commentaries of Burgin's *US 77*. McLuhan reprints, and comments on, advertisements and strip cartoons taken from the American press over this period. Burgin, travelling throughout the United States a quarter of a century later, picks up images on roadside hoardings and in densely populated city streets that are astonishingly reminiscent of McLuhan's array. The kind of sexist advertisement which McLuhan amusingly dubs the 'Love Goddess Assembly Line' is rediscovered by Burgin, with the feminine figures transformed in accordance with the latest Hollywood model, by the side of a desolate suburban roadway.

2. A.L.Rees and F. Borzello, *The New Art History*, London: Camden Press, 1986.

Yet this is to notice very little except what both Burgin and McLuhan implicitly accept: that is, the recycling of such stereotypes in accordance with the economic and social demands of mass society. When we begin to look at the differences between them, it is first of all the very stance of the cultural critic that is at stake. McLuhan, with his academic basis in the study of Shakespeare and the classics of English literature, views the modern world as a whirlpool from which the critic must, imperatively, act to rescue himself. In fact, he takes as his leading example the story by Edgar Allan Poe entitled *Descent into the Maelstrom*, in which the narrator describes in enormous detail the rational calculation which enabled him to escape from the deadly vortex of the raging ocean. There can scarcely be any doubt that he is anxious about the condition of the modern world, and the witty and insightful comments that he makes upon the contemporary churning of clichés are predicated upon this need to set himself apart from it. Burgin's road movie, *US 77*, does not claim to carry such inherited baggage.

A cultural critic who is closer in date and in spirit to Burgin's enterprise is, of course, Roland Barthes. In his *Mythologies*, initially published in 1957, Barthes moved adroitly through the different zones of French urban culture in the last years of the nation's colonial entanglement, picking up the evidence of Hollywood's ubiquitous revision of the classics ('The Romans in Film') as much as the local  fetishes of wrestling matches and steak and chips. But there is one crucial aspect that differentiates Barthes from McLuhan, with his copious if somewhat grainy reproductions of the images under discussion. Barthes never includes an image. Indeed, in the famous case of the 'young black soldier saluting the flag' in the closing essay on 'Myth Today', it now seems undeniable that a publication of the image would have unsettled the whole analysis. The actual cover of *Paris-Match* that is under discussion hardly bears the inference that Barthes places upon it. But this is not, I suggest, inadvertence or shoddy criticism on Barthes's part. On the contrary, the scenario of seeing the cover at the barber's shop – and therefore only casually – is crucial to Barthes's argument about the colonialist subconscious of the average French person. To have singled out the image and presented it to the reader pedagogically as a formal object of study would have been to destroy the persona that Barthes had adopted in *Mythologies*: as a *flâneur* through whom the codes of the city washed back and forth leaving only the trace of an *ad hoc* response.

Following pages: *US 77*, 1977, twelve sections, each 100 x 150 cm

PATRIARCHITECTURE
The man almost always feels his sexual activity hampered by his respect for the woman. Hence comes his need for a less exalted sexual object, a woman ethically inferior, to whom he need ascribe no aesthetic misgivings, and who does not know the rest of his life and cannot criticize him. It is to such a woman that he prefers to devote his sexual potency, even when all the tenderness in him belongs to one of a higher type. It has an ugly and paradoxical sound, but nevertheless it must be said that whoever is to be really free and happy in love must have overcome his deference for women and come to terms with the idea of incest with mother or sister.

FOUR-WORD LOOKING
Times change, values don't.
They speak from experience,
forgetting that in remembering
as much is lost as found.
Because they don't know what they've lost
they think they've won.

This argument may seem to be leading up to the rather obvious point that Burgin is an artist, unlike McLuhan or Barthes, because he selects images and exhibits them in galleries. But the fact that there is indeed a product to be shown – not a mere illustration as with McLuhan, and not an ambiguous veiled referent as with Barthes – is itself contingent upon the particular kind of intervention which the artist decides to make. Burgin himself has confessed to having had concerns

about the degree to which his strategies as a photographer might be confused with the activist commitment of a certain strand of documentary photography. In an interview for *Block* in 1982, he referred to one episode in his earlier career as being 'if not actually exploitative . . . politically irrelevant'. But in a later comment on that particular interview, he confessed to having reached a more agnostic position:

I no longer have such a 'negative' view of such photographic interventions. Some are useful, others not – only specific circumstances decide, and it is wrong to generalise. However I would still say it is particularly wrong to make the sort of generalisation which automatically assumes that the photographer in this sort of situation is politically useful.[3]

3. Victor Burgin, *Between*, Oxford: Blackwell, 1986, p. 39.

Quite apart from this, one might reasonably say that, in Burgin's case, the structure of the presentation encourages ambiguity and indeterminacy on the level of image-text relationship, which is not a feature either of cultural criticism or of documentary photography. In this respect, he is being faithful to the commitment, from the already quoted passage: 'to dismantle existing communication codes and to recombine some of their elements into structures which can be used to generate new pictures of the world'. In *US 77*, this approach is paradigmatically represented by the short capitalised 'titles' which use word-play and overdetermined metaphor: NUCLEAR POWER, OMNIMPOTENCE, PHALLACY and PENNIS FROM HEAVEN. Supplemented as they are with short texts that include two from Freud, these titles signal the photographic image as a kind of visible dream text, or a hieroglyph as Freud might have called it. The juxtapositions are often extremely witty, as with the 'nuclear' family completed by a handy moonwalker, or the Italian grocer exposing his monster salami against the sky. But they are not mere witticisms. For example, the utterly charming informality of the family group photographed in NUCLEAR POWER is complemented by a strict metric text from a traditional English collection: 'The father gives his kind command, / mother joins, approves; / the children all attentive stand, / then each obedient moves.' The superficial contrast is striking, but then we

begin to think again about the activity of visiting a space museum: here is a routine no less constraining than the drill of the attentive children, in relation to which the model of the moonwalker (but is it a model?) might suggest a futile fantasy of escape. Oddly enough, as we notice, the striped top of the 'mother' seems to 'rhyme' with the stripes of the American flag, while the flash-bulbs protruding from her camera could almost be taking the place of the stars. This might recall the flag symbolism used to stir up demand for commodities with a patriotic connotation in one of McLuhan's adverts. But the address to the audience is, of course, very different.

I hardly have to say much more to prove that Burgin's role as an artist, rather than a cultural critic, is to favour rather than close off the chains of connotation. There is no 'punch-line' as there may often be in McLuhan, or indeed Barthes. The temporality of our reception is also different, as the image reveals itself very slowly, even when accompanied by a text that has the character of a prompt. Here the use of quotations from Freud is a significant pointer, since it betokens a more radical reorientation of Burgin's work which indeed took place in the mid-1970s, shortly before the production of US 77. As Burgin himself states: 'It represents the point in my work at which a certain kind of feminist argument overcame my residual economistic Marxism. The construction of sexual difference in representation becomes the issue.' He adds as a rider to this retrospective judgement: 'This is the point at which, for certain friends on the left, my work started to go astray.'[4]

4. Ibid., p. 40.

Burgin was not, of course, alone in appearing to some to go astray at this particular point in time. What is perhaps interesting, in view of the comment made in 1973 about assessing an artist in terms of cinema, is the fact that he chose in broad terms to share the reorientation which was simultaneously taking place in film studies in Britain, as a result of the activity around the British Film Institute journal, *Screen*, and which resulted in the introduction of film as an academic subject in a number of British universities. There was no inevitability about this alliance between the theoretical concerns of cinema and those of art. In France, over the same period, the

practices of cinema and media-related art were not conjoined in any such common programme. Indeed the diverse group of writers and critics around the magazine *Tel Quel*, which most closely mirrored the theoretical concerns of the group around *Screen* in the 1970s, gave its backing to the Supports/Surfaces group of abstract painters. In Britain, Burgin's development led to him standing virtually alone in the generation which had pioneered conceptualism. Among the artists of the Art & Language group, for example, Anglo-American analytic philosophy, and especially the ideas of Wittgenstein, held unquestioned primacy. For Burgin, as the second part of the Commentary to *Work and Commentary* already bore witness in 1973, this place was taken by the legacy of Saussure: structuralism and semiology.

Yet there is already at this stage a dimension to Burgin's work that decisively supplements and conditions his concern with signs and codes. One of his earliest published writings was an essay originally published in *Studio International* in 1969, under the title 'Situational Aesthetics'. Jennifer Gonzalez was right to give this statement considerable weight in her informative discussion of the concept of 'Installation Art', which she sees as being derived from manifold sources in the history of the European and American avant-garde. Burgin's special contribution, in her view, is the replacement of the notion of art as 'a material, fabricated object' by 'a set of *conditions* for the demonstration of concepts, or *systems* that might generate objects – in short, *situations*.'[5] At the time when this essay was written, and for a year or two afterwards, Burgin was producing mainly text works, and *Performative/Narrative* (1971) is one of the rare examples of the introduction of a photograph which is repeated with minute variations. However, all of these texts, whether or not supplemented by an image, are concerned with setting up a 'situation' that is defined in terms of the attention and memory of the person who reads them. They therefore support the implication, as Gonzalez puts it, that 'the artist may be less interested in the creation of new material forms . . . than in the coordination or reorganisation of existing forms.'

A surprising connection may be suggested here with another development carried out by British artists of Burgin's generation, who are not often considered as

5. Jennifer Gonzalez, 'Installation Art', in Michael Kelly (ed.), *Encyclopaedia of Aesthetics*, Oxford: Oxford University Press, 1998, vol. 2, p. 506.

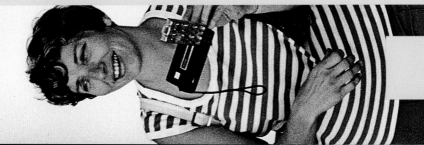

belonging within the same context. British land artists, such as Richard Long and Hamish Fulton, began around 1970 to negotiate the complementary 'situations' of the gallery and the landscape, using non-intrusive methods to imprint their marks upon nature, and often relying on the photograph to provide a lasting index of a fugitive effect of intervention. To mention them is, however, to recognise that a possible similarity in strategy masks a fundamental difference in artistic orientation. For Long and Fulton, the 'land' is what may be explored by the individual walker; it is not necessarily uncontaminated nature, and it is certainly not devoid of any cultural or ethnographic traces. But the contract of the artist with the spectator remains in essence that of the traditional landscape artist, developed at the same time as the landscape genre consolidated itself from the eighteenth century onwards. The artist, self-delegated, returns from his travels to convey to us the sense of the sublime. Burgin, even when he travels, shows us the tissues of the urban culture that we already know. Of his contemporaries, perhaps only Stephen Willats has kept a comparably vigilant eye on the changing industrial townscape. But

Performative Narrative 1971, sixteen sections, each 34 x 67 cm

Willats works like a genre artist, essentially concerned with complicated human interactions in a contemporary milieu crowded with objects. With Burgin, the uncanny is never far from the surface.

Take, for example, the image of the two young women who advance a little warily towards us along a sunlit street in the first triptych of his sequence, *In Lyon* (1980). They look alike, and are dressed in a very similar fashion. One has a slightly more plunging neckline and carries her sun-glasses attached to the v-neck of her jumper. Their bags and their wrist watches are clearly different. Are these cousins, or sisters, or maybe twins? In any event, they are not thrust into our faces by the photographer, like some of the ghoulish pairs photographed by Diane Arbus. They are gracefully at one with the fashionable street, perhaps out to cover the *Soldes* (Sales) whose products are temptingly visible through the plate-glass window. Yet their doubleness lends them a slightly disturbing, fantasmatic quality in this concrete, everyday setting.

If I differentiate the way in which these image/text sequences affect us from the familiar strategies of the contemporary photographer, this is not in any sense to repudiate photography's more long-term heritage. It seems to me that, on the contrary, Burgin takes us back to a stage when photography was ready to assume more ambitious tasks, precisely because its techniques were still openly experimental. Looking at the image which is paired with the two young women in the Lyon street, I recall the writings of the great nineteenth-century photographer Nadar, whose desire to reach technical mastery in the rapidly evolving medium was sometimes qualified by a pungent critique of the other artistic media that competed for public attention in the streets of Paris. Describing one assignment in the Rue Richelieu, he recounts that it took place opposite the fountain erected by the sculptor Pradier, of whom a colleague had remarked: 'He leaves every morning for Athens, and he returns every evening to Place Bréda.'[6]

6. Nadar, *Quand j'étais photographe*, Paris: Seuil, new edition, 1994, p. 141.

This ironic reference to the admired public sculptor who aspires to classical excellence, but reverts all too soon to the bourgeois taste of his times, strikes me as comparable to the way in which Burgin profiles the languid public statuary of Lyon against the prim apartment building with its ornamental balconies. Nadar's writings leave us with an unforgettable impression that photography can open up the city in the way that no other medium can claim to do: it will reveal to us its sublime heights and its squalid depths, and permit us to look its myriad inhabitants straight in the eye. Burgin does not have to reckon, as Nadar did, with the defects of a medium still to be tuned to the photographer's vision: 'eyeballs blotted out by an excess of brightness or brutally pricked, like two nails.' But, in using the perfected technical apparatus of contemporary photography, he does not forgo the critical ambition of the earlier period, or relinquish the original project of discovery.

Yet, if Nadar's mapping of the city suggests a possible precedent for much of Burgin's work from 1980 onwards, this is a cartography that is invariably animated by the projections of desire. The second pair of images in the Lyon sequence is wonderfully clear in its binary oppositions, both within and between the content of the two views. On the one hand, there is a historical scene without actors: the abraded Corinthian capital that marks the age-old standing of Lyon as an important Roman city is balanced by the functional modern hand-rail that frames a modern apartment block. No ghosts seem to be walking here.

Nevertheless, if we shift our attention to the other image, the reflective surfaces of an office building in the new quarter of La Part-Dieu seem to dematerialise the interior space, and make the striding figure almost as much of a hieroglyphic sign as the stark contemporary sculpture in the background. We have seen this figure before, and will see it again in Burgin's detail from a photograph taken in Warsaw in 1981, later to be reproduced on the cover of *Some Cities*. Each is a version of the *Gradiva*, or stepping woman, whose image moulded after a classical relief hung in Freud's consulting room, and became the pretext for Wilhelm Jensen's lengthy disquisition on the modern story.[7] Georges Didi-Huberman has recently written of this figure almost as the emblem of Freud's psychoanalytic method: 'As if this young creature from fiction succeeded in making analytic knowledge . . . into a kind of exercise in disturbing charm, with memory and desire being brought together in the same apparition.'[8]

I have spent some time looking at *In Lyon* because it seems to me to mark a significant intersection in Burgin's development. Together with its close successor *In Grenoble* (1981), it marks the point at which the objective of a 'situational aesthetics', and its relation to the work of cultural critics like McLuhan and Barthes, are simultaneously clarified. *In Grenoble* seems to play some of the same sequences as *In Lyon* but, as it were, in a different key. The double female image here relates to the industrial past of the city, and the plaintive greenery of a new suburb echoes the idyllic image of a landscape by Claude which is exhibited in the local museum. Arcadian shepherds step out in the Claudian scene, while, in the second, a contemporary mother and daughter stride with self-confident purpose against the silhouettes of distant mountains and nearby workers' flats. It seems appropriate that directly after these two works, in 1982, Gradiva should come into her own. Burgin devoted a sequence of seven panels to the pairing of his fragmentary retelling of the Gradiva story with haunting images, including the original scene of the Warsaw encounter excerpted for the cover of *Some Cities*.

7. 'Delusions and Dreams in Jensen's "Gradiva"', in Sigmund Freud, *Art and Literature*, Harmondsworth: Penguin, 1985, pp. 33-109.

8. Georges Didi-Huberman, *Ninfa moderna – Essai sur le drapé tombé*, Paris: Gallimard, 2002, p. 8.

In Lyon
1980, three triptychs, each panel
50 x 66 cm

To come right up to date with Burgin's critical topography would involve a further scrutiny of the new media that he has continued to develop. But just as I prefer to focus on the example of Nadar as embodying the kinship between technical research and critical objectives, so I find another nineteenth-century example helpful in giving a broader historical context to an important strand of his work. In his essay on 'John Ruskin', the young Proust exclaimed: 'What an interesting collection might be made of French landscapes as seen through English eyes . . .'[9] Proust then goes on to mention several examples of what might feature in such a collection: 'the rivers of France by Turner; Bonington's "Versailles"; Walter Pater's "Auxerre" or "Valenciennes", "Vézelay" or "Amiens"; Stevenson's "Fontainebleau"; and how many more!' Several of these are, of course, literary landscapes, with Turner and Bonington being the obvious exceptions. But Proust's reference to Ruskin's *Bible of Amiens* implies both image and text working together, since Ruskin inserted his own engravings in the analysis of the city and its cathedral. Proust comments on this visual element, while bearing the textual message constantly in mind:

But at least this engraving . . . will have associated the banks of the Somme and the cathedral more closely together in your memory than your eyes no doubt could have done; no matter at

what point in the town you had been placed. It will prove to you better than anything I can have said that Ruskin made no separation between the beauty of the cathedrals and the charm of the country out of which they arose . . .

Displaced from an aesthetic into a critical mode, Burgin's image/text works are also reliant on the memory to deepen the casual encounters of the eye. Their sustained interweaving of content and context depends on the image's unique capacity to condense and combine meanings.

9. Marcel Proust, *Against Sainte-Beuve and other essays*, translated by John Sturrock, London: Penguin, 1988, p. 176.

Everywhere, or not at all
Victor Burgin and conceptual art

Peter Osborne

Contemporary art is routinely derided for being 'conceptual'. Yet most of what passes as conceptual in the art of the last ten years has little relation to that more rigorously intellectual body of work from the 1960s and early 1970s that gave conceptual art its name. This essay reconsiders Victor Burgin's work from the standpoint of its relationship to conceptual art. Conversely, it reflects on the significance of Burgin's work for the idea of conceptual art. For it is still a matter of some dispute precisely how best to characterise it. Taken as a whole, I shall suggest, Burgin's art throws new light on the legacy of conceptual art in current art practices, light that reflects back and illuminates the critical meaning of Burgin's own most recent works.

Burgin's early work, 1967–72, is usually taken to form a discrete, artistically self-sufficient 'conceptual' period, prior to the political photo-texts of the mid-1970s and the elegantly austere psychoanalytical works of the 1980s, for which he is best known. Yet there has been little consideration of either the specific place of these early works within conceptual art in Britain and North America or their relations to Burgin's subsequent practice. This has affected the reception of Burgin's art in two main ways. First, it has left the early work prey to the philosophical and linguistic reductionism of the critically hegemonic version of conceptual art, from which it was, in fact, self-consciously distanced from the outset. Second, it has left interpretation of the 'post-conceptual' photographic works overly dependent upon the theoretical terms of those of Burgin's writings that are immediately contemporary with them (and which, indeed, appear to 'explain' them). The dialectical continuity of Burgin's artistic development has thus been doubly obscured. In contrast, I shall suggest that Burgin's move to a politicised photographic art practice is best understood not as the rejection of a primarily conceptual art, but as the practical pursuit of its expanded conception.

Contextual art

Art is primarily a situation
Robert Morris, 'Blank Form' (1960–61)

Burgin's early works and writings, from *Photopath* (1967–69) and 'Situational Aesthetics' (1969) to *Work and Commentary* (1973) and 'In Reply' (1972) show him in artistic and critical dialogue with a range of tendencies within the diverse and experimental field of the art of the day. Foremost among these were the process-based forms of contextual art that had emerged out of the competing minimalisms of Donald Judd, Robert Morris and Sol LeWitt, on the one hand, and the more explicitly philosophical or 'analytical' conceptual art of Joseph Kosuth and Art & Language, on the other. Burgin's writings between 1969 and 1972 may be read as an attempt to elaborate a conceptual version of the former in opposition to the 'hermeticism' of the latter, while nonetheless engaging with the latter on its own favoured, philosophical terrain.[1]

1. In so doing, Burgin was mediating his recent experience in the USA, as a graduate student in the School of Art and Architecture at Yale (1965–67), with the British art scene. This was a role played at a more general level by the journal *Studio International*, in which a number of Burgin's early essays first appeared. For a discussion of the attraction of conceptual artists to academic philosophy, in its then-dominant analytical mode (with particular reference to LeWitt, Kosuth and Art & Language), see Peter Osborne,'Conceptual Art and/as Philosophy', in Michael Newman and Jon Bird (eds.), *Rewriting Conceptual Art*, London: Reaktion Books, pp. 47–65.

'Situational Aesthetics' was published in the same issue of *Studio International* (October 1969) as the first part of Kosuth's contentious three-part article, 'Art After Philosophy'. Burgin's essay opens with a symbolic contrast between two manifestations of a tendency common to some recent art 'to take its essential form in message rather than in materials': a 'logically extreme' and 'hermetic' variety that 'has resulted in a placing of art entirely within the linguistic infrastructure which previously served merely to support art' (for which, read Seth Siegelaub and Art & Language); and a less logicist variety (for which, read Burgin himself, among others) in which 'art as message, as "software", consists of sets of conditions, more or less closely defined, according to which particular concepts may be demonstrated'. This conception of art as the activity of *defining sets of conditions* for the demonstration of particular concepts is further elaborated as the design of 'aesthetic *systems* . . . capable of generating objects, rather than individual objects themselves'. (Aesthetic systems may be understood here as sets of rules governing the formation of objects in perception out of the matrix or flux of space-time.) The emphasis is thus on process, rather than the resultant objects, and hence upon 'objects' in an expanded, phenomenological

Photopath, 1967

sense that includes the systems through which perceptual objects are generated as themselves 'conceptual objects'.[2]

The artistic significance of materials (medium) is reduced to their productive, communicational or signifying functions (message). However, there is no attempt to restrict art to linguistic materials, since it remains 'aesthetic', in the classical sense of working via spatio-temporal aspects of perceptual objects. Nonetheless, this aesthetic dimension functions primarily negatively, directing attention away from itself towards conceptual structures of perception:

Any attempt to make an 'object' of non-overt and insubstantial conceptual forms demands that substantial materials located in exterior space-time be used in a manner which subverts their 'objectness' in order to identify them as 'situational cues'.

Conversely, Burgin argued, conceptual elements are themselves 'to some extent [to] be conceived of, and accounted for, through analogy with the experience of substantial elements' – principally by kinaesthetic analogy, in terms of the body. There is therefore a dual dependence of this kind of conceptual art on material objectivity, as both analogy and self-negating ground. But its specific modes of dependence effect a 'reversal of function' between materials and their context. It is this reversal of function – by which materials become situational cues for conceptual interpretations of perception – that Burgin summed up in the phrase 'situational aesthetics'.[3]

Burgin conceived this kind of art as 'a redirection of attention, from object to perceiver'.[4] Given its expansion of the concept of an object, however, we might think of it as an exploration of the dual, conceptual and perceptual, aspects of objects of experience. As such, it registers the affinity of Burgin's variant of conceptual art at this time with the work of Morris and LeWitt, and also Mel Bochner and Adrian Piper.[5] This is apparent in the works by Burgin that provide the illustrations for his essay of 1969: *Photopath* (in two different installations from 1969), *Memory Piece* (1969) and *25 ft two hours* (1969).

2. Victor Burgin, 'Situational Aesthetics', *Studio International*, vol. 178, no. 915, October 1969, pp. 118–121. Phenomenology concerns itself with that directedness towards objects that constitute the subject as a conscious being, irrespective of the ontological properties of the objects themselves. In the phenomenological sense, an 'object' is thus anything which is 'for a subject'.

3. Ibid.

4. Ibid., p. 121, note 4.

5. See the section on 'Process, System, Series' in Peter Osborne, *Conceptual Art*, London: Phaidon, 2002, pp. 23–26. Like LeWitt, Burgin at this time tends to identify the 'conceptual' with *psychological* space. This tendency to psychological reductionism persists in Burgin's more recent writings in his use of the Freudian conception of 'psychical space'; specifically, in the idea that 'th[e] distinction between the social and the psychical …is …an abstraction, a fantasy.' (Victor Burgin, *In/Different Spaces: Place and Memory in Visual Culture*, Berkeley, Los Angeles and London: California University Press, 1996, p. 36) However, that the two are mutually constitutive does not erase the conceptual distinction between them.

Photopath involves a radicalisation of the minimalist conception of negative space, via the attenuation of the 'positive' object that generates such space to the point of the *imagined* elimination of the perceptual distinction between the object and its context/environment. As such, it marks the transition from a sculptural to a more fully conceptual conception of the contextual character of artistic meaning.[6] More particularly, it exploits the indexicality of the photographic image in order to use it as a sign of perceptual indifference. The photographs function to 'select' a portion of the environment (a section of the floor), rather than being valued for the independent material or figural qualities of their representational form. The elimination is only tendential (one might say, horizonal), however, since the piece requires a residual perceptual – and hence material – distinction between the photographs and the floor around them as the basis for the relation of similarity that signifies the *idea* of perceptual indifference. Photography thus functions here as a new kind of blank form.[7]

Equally important to the conceptual functioning of the piece is the fact that *Photopath* is reproducible, in the sense of having an infinite number of possible instantiations. It is reproducible, however, *not* primarily because of its photographic nature (each instance of which will be different, because 'adapted' to a different spatial context), but rather because of the linguistic character of its 'definition of a set of conditions'. Here, reproducibility derives from the universality inherent in language, rather than from the technical features of photography. The caption to the second photograph of the piece in *Studio International* reads:

A path along the floor, of proportions 1 x 21 units, photographed. Photographs printed to actual size of objects and prints stapled to the floor so that images are perfectly congruent with their objects.

The catalogue for Burgin's exhibition at the Fundació Antoni Tàpies (April–June 2001) describes this text as an 'instruction' – in fact, it reproduces it (with one minor variation) as an 'instruction card' dated 1967.[8] However, the term 'instruction' is misleading here; although it does draw attention to the trace in this work of the performative character of the earliest (proto-Fluxus) works of

6. Cf. The gradual attenuation in the role of the object in Robert Morris's 'Notes on Sculpture' from 'Part I', *Artforum*, February 1966, through to 'Part IV: Beyond Objects', April 1969; reprinted in Robert Morris, *Continuous Project Altered Daily: The Writings of Robert Morris*, Cambridge MA and London: MIT Press, 1993, pp. 1–39 and 51–70. However, Morris himself stopped short of a fully conceptual interpretation. Morris taught at the Yale School of Art and Architecture during Burgin's period there as a graduate student. See 'Interview with Victor Burgin', in John Roberts (ed.), *The Impossible Document: Photography and Conceptual Art in Britain, 1966–1976*, London: Camerawork, 1997, pp. 80–103.

7. Robert Morris, 'Blank Form' (1960–61), reprinted in the Documents section of Osborne, op. cit., p.195. Morris wrote this brief text for La Monte Young's proto-Fluxus collection, *An Anthology*, but withdrew it before the book appeared in 1963.

8. *Victor Burgin*, Barcelona: Fundació Antoni Tàpies, 2001, p. 56. In place of the word 'stapled' in the *Studio International* caption, this version has the more generic 'attached'.

Photopath
1969, ICA, London

67

conceptual art from 1961–62, with their background in music and dance, mediated in all likelihood by the work of Morris.[9] It is misleading because this 'definition of a set of conditions' is in the same past tense and passive voice as Lawrence Weiner's 'Statements', which Weiner explicitly contrasts with the 'tone of tyranny' of the imperative, the 'command' form of instruction-works. Despite the past tense, the passive voice renders the objects of such statements temporally indeterminate. The time of such works is thus to be distinguished from both the orientation towards the future characteristic of instruction-works and the active pastness of documentary works alike (although they have documented instances). These works are open to the possibility of future realisations, but as Weiner's famous 'Statement of Intent' about his own work points out: 'The piece need not be built.'[10] Indeed, many of Burgin's index-card works from 1967 have never been fabricated.

Photopath shares with Weiner's works the same, distinctively conceptual mode of existence. Both enjoy the ideal distributive unity of an infinite totality of possible realisations, of which there are nonetheless certain historically privileged actual instances, at the levels of both linguistic articulation and fabricated form. Indeed, the linguistic articulation will itself, of necessity, always take a particular material form.[11] Weiner was interested in language as a sculptural material. For Burgin, on the other hand, here the text functions visually in a more neutral manner, as the means of specification of conceptual content, and although it is in this respect the key articulating element of the work, it is not a visually marked element of its material form. In retaining the conventional scale and relative visual neutrality of the print culture of the book, it 'subverts its own objectness' by appearing to belong to a different order of information: the 'secondary information' of gallery commentary that might be expected to accompany, rather than itself to be a part of, the work.[12]

9. See the section on 'Instruction, Performance, Documentation' in Osborne, op. cit., pp. 19–23.

10. John Anthony Thwaites, 'Lawrence Weiner: An Interview and An Interpretation', *Art and Artists*, August 1972, p. 23; quoted in Alexander Alberro and Alice Zimmerman, 'Not How It Should Were It To Be Built But How It Could Were It To Be Built', in Alexander Alberro et al, *Lawrence Weiner*, London: Phaidon, 1998, p. 49. Weiner's Statements were first published as a book in 1968. The 'Statement of Intent', which would henceforth accompany Weiner's works, was first published in the catalogue for the show *January 5–13, 1969*, New York. 'Statements' was reprinted in the British journal *Art-Language: The Journal of Conceptual Art*, vol. 1, no. 1, May 1969, pp. 17–18, the editorial 'Introduction' to which Burgin refers in 'Situational Aesthetics' in his opening remarks, distancing himself from Art & Language, who at this time posited theory as itself a possible form of art.

11. Cf. Osborne op. cit., pp. 30–32. For an exposition of the concept of distributive unity, and its application at the level of a cultural form (rather than an individual work), see Peter Osborne, 'Photography in an Expanding Field: Distributive Unity and Dominant Form', in David Green (ed.), *Photography/Philosophy/Technology*, Brighton: Photoforum/Photoworks, 2002.

12. For the distinction between primary and secondary information, and the idea that in conceptual art traditionally secondary forms, such as the catalogue, can become primary (i.e. the site of the work itself), see Seth Siegelaub, interview with Ursula Meyer, 19 November 1969, in Lucy Lippard, *Six Years: The Dematerialization of the Art Object from 1966 to 1972*, Berkeley: California University Press, 1973, 2nd ed. 1997, pp. 124–26.

Furthermore, the conceptual content of *Photopath* remains preoccupied with perception, rather than inscription, or the relationship between inscription, conception/imagining and fabricated form. This is equally true of the text works that follow (1970–72), despite the fact that, unlike the three works realised in 1969 illustrating 'Situational Aesthetics', they do not involve specifications of forms that might be fabricated. At this time, Burgin was using language as an artistic means for investigating conceptual structures of perception, rather than as either a model of meaning in general (as it was for Kosuth) or a self-sufficient artistic form (as it was used by Art & Language). It was this continuing orientation towards perception that would lead Terry Atkinson and Michael Baldwin of Art & Language to accuse Burgin of attempting 'to turn language into paint'.[13] In clarifying his differences from Art & Language, Burgin was led to a decisive reformulation – and radical expansion – of his conception of art that took his practice in a new and now familiar direction.

13. Terry Atkinson and Michael Baldwin, 'Unnatural Rules and Excuses', *Art-Language*, vol. 2, no. 1, February 1972, p. 21.

A conceptual aesthetic

Burgin's text works from 1970 to 1972 – such as *Room*, *Any Moment* and *All Criteria* (all from 1970) and *IV 2* (1972) – perform a reflective mediation of the phenomenological concerns of a post-minimalist contextual art with the philosophico-linguistic and set-theoretical problematic of analytical conceptualism. *Room* is a text work for display on the wall of a gallery space. More specifically, *Room* is a serial conceptual construction of eighteen propositions based on two foundational indexical designations: one spatial – '1 All substantial things which constitute this room' – the other, temporal – '3 The present moment and only the present moment'. The other sixteen propositions are increasingly complex designations that specify particular aspects of possible experience within the parameters of the two foundational spatio-temporal denotations: from '4 All appearances of 1 directly experienced by you at 3' to '18 Any member of 16 which you consider in whole or in part analogous with any member of 12' – where propositions 16 and 12 designate aspects of experience that are themselves specified with reference to previous propositions in the series.[14]

14. The second proposition in the series, to which no further reference is made – '2 All the duration of 1' – is something of an anomaly. It marks an awkwardness or philosophical uncertainty about the relationship between the ontological discourse of 'substantial things' and the phenomenological discourse of the 'present moment'. It appears redundant, since the phenomenological character of the 'this' in 1 ('All substantial things which constitute this room') is already implicitly durational. [Note: There is a setting error in the version of the work reproduced in the Tàpies Foundation catalogue, in proposition 16 it should conclude with the repetition of proposition 3, not proposition 1.]

On the one hand, the textual form of *Room* 'subverts [its] "objectness" in order to identify [it] as [a] situational cue'. This effect is internally reinforced by its use of

0
ANY MOMENT PREVIOUS TO
THE PRESENT MOMENT

1
THE PRESENT MOMENT AND
ONLY THE PRESENT MOMENT

2
ALL APPARENTLY INDIVIDUAL
OBJECTS DIRECTLY EXPERIENCED
BY YOU AT 1

3
ALL OF YOUR RECOLLECTION AT 1
OF APPARENTLY INDIVIDUAL OBJECTS
DIRECTLY EXPERIENCED BY YOU AT
0 AND KNOWN TO BE IDENTICAL
WITH 2

4
ALL CRITERIA BY WHICH YOU MIGHT
DISTINGUISH BETWEEN MEMBERS OF 3
AND 2

5
ALL OF YOUR EXTRAPOLATION FROM
2 AND 3 CONCERNING THE DISPOSITION
OF 2 AT 0

6
ALL ASPECTS OF THE DISPOSITION
OF YOUR OWN BODY AT 1 WHICH
YOU CONSIDER IN WHOLE OR IN
PART STRUCTURALLY ANALOGOUS
WITH THE DISPOSITION OF 2

7
ALL OF YOUR INTENTIONAL BODILY
ACTS PERFORMED UPON ANY MEMBER
OF 2

8
ALL OF YOUR BODILY SENSATIONS
WHICH YOU CONSIDER CONTINGENT
UPON YOUR BODILY CONTACT WITH
ANY MEMBER OF 2

9
ALL EMOTIONS DIRECTLY EXPERIENCED
BY YOU AT 1

10
ALL OF YOUR BODILY SENSATIONS
WHICH YOU CONSIDER CONTINGENT
UPON ANY MEMBER OF 9

11
ALL CRITERIA BY WHICH YOU MIGHT
DISTINGUISH BETWEEN MEMBERS OF
10 AND OF 8

12
ALL OF YOUR RECOLLECTION AT 1
OTHER THAN 3

13
ALL ASPECTS OF 12 UPON WHICH
YOU CONSIDER ANY MEMBER OF 9
TO BE CONTINGENT

what linguists call 'shifters' or indexical terms (such as 'this') that refer the viewer to the phenomenological here-and-now of the space-time in which the work is installed (originally, in 1970, in Camden Arts Centre). Attention is drawn to the conceptual structure of the viewer/reader's perception of the room in which they are located. On the other hand, however, the accumulative articulation of internal relations between the eighteen numbered propositions, gives *Room* something of the appearance of a parody of Wittgenstein's *Tractatus Logico-Philosophicus*, by gesturing towards a kind of logical self-sufficiency or completeness. In fact, logical completeness functions here in much the same way as perceptual indifference does in *Photopath*: namely, as an idea produced by, and regulating, the experience of the work. In its conceptual generality, *Room* transcends the phenomenological context to which it refers in any given instance, by its very means of reference (language) – just as *Photopath* has a conceptual content that both transcends and encompasses its particular instantiations. Each work thereby sets up a dialectic between the perceptual and the conceptual that is internal to its conceptual content.[15]

On the page, today, alienated from its context of installation, its words comfortably re-installed in the familiar form of the book, *Room* looks much like some works of the same period by Art & Language – and, Burgin's work was, at this time, associated with that of Art & Language, if only by default, via their mutual relations to the curator and editor of *Studio International*, Charles Harrison.[16] But the differences run deep. *Room*'s propositions are not part of an 'enquiry into the language-use of the art society'.[17] They are cues for reflective mental acts that register aspects of an existential state: being-in-the-room. Moreover, this mode of being-in-the-room – reflective attention to perception – is that of the institutionally dominant, aesthetic conception of the experience of the artwork. *Room* accepts, and manipulates, its institutional conditions of existence: display in a gallery space. Initially, it frustrates the viewer's expectations – there are, apparently, no art objects, only text – but then it fulfils them, albeit in a new way, thereby

15. Such stagings of the relations between 'subjective' and 'objective' systems of reference are also at the heart of early works by Adrian Piper, such as *Here and Now* (1968). It is interesting that Piper, setting out from LeWitt, and Burgin, setting out from Morris, should have developed such parallel practices. They are also, not unrelatedly, both artists whose work would subsequently become directly political.

16. Burgin's *Photopath* was one of the works Harrison added to the show *When Attitudes Become Form* when it travelled from the Kunsthalle, Berne, to the Institute of Contemporary Arts, London, in 1969. Harrison curated *Idea Structures* at Camden Arts Centre, at which *Room* was first shown, along with works by Art & Language. He was also one of six 'curators' of the special Book Supplement of *Studio International*, July/August 1970, each of whom commissioned a separate section of the journal. Harrison's section included Burgin along with work by four members of Art & Language, among others. Burgin has attributed Harrison with 'single-handedly [giving] conceptual art a platform in England' at this time ('Interview', p. 87), prior to Harrison becoming the 'General Editor' of *Art-Language* from vol. 2, no. 2, summer 1972, onwards. This was the issue in which Burgin's 'In Reply' summed up his fundamental disagreement with the Art & Language project. Harrison subsequently became the critical sponsor and official historian of Art & Language.

17. Introduction, *Art-Language*, vol. 1, no. 1, p. 10.

Any Moment, 1970

demonstrating that art can be made out of the mere designation of objects of perception. This is a new reflexive – one might say 'conceptual' – aesthetic.

Contextual art has a conceptual aesthetic: it draws attention to the conceptual aspects of perception and, thereby, to the conceptual character of the subject's very mode of being in the world. In Burgin's terms from the time (borrowed from the logical positivist philosopher Rudolf Carnap), art is 'a fundamentally *apperceptive* operation'.[18] It works on the subject's affective relation to itself. Yet 'analytical' conceptual artists, such as Kosuth and Art & Language, directly opposed the conceptual (which they understood in narrowly linguistic terms as the propositional) to the aesthetic and the affective. Burgin was thus led to contest the propositional self-sufficiency of the self-understanding of analytical conceptual art, declaring that 'art *has* no language';[19] and to characterise the exclusive concern with the meaning of 'art' in analytical conceptualism as 'a recasting of *l'art pour l'art*'.[20] In contrast, he argued:

18. Victor Burgin, 'Rules of Thumb', *Studio International*, vol. 181, no. 933, May 1971, pp. 237–39 – reprinted in Alexander Alberro and Blake Stimson, *Conceptual Art: A Critical Anthology*, Cambridge MA and London: MIT Press, 1999, pp. 248–55. Apperception is a term used philosophically (following Leibniz and Kant) to refer to a subject's awareness of itself, as opposed to perception, which denotes a subject's awareness of an object in space.

Art's primary situation is not unique to art. It is that in which a person, or group of persons, by certain displays, seeks to alter the state of apprehension of a second person or group of persons.[21]

The central and 'consistently ignored' aspect of '"the problem of legitimation" in art' is thus the question – not of art's meaning, but – of 'art's *use*.'[22]

However, this move away from an immanent investigation of the contextual character of artistic meaning to a preoccupation with art's use should not be understood as a move away from 'conceptual art'. Rather, it represents the progressive articulation of a distinctive position *within* its discursive field. For Burgin's conception of the artwork as a message carried by sensuous materials remained essentially unchanged. This continuity is disguised by the contrast between the 'analytical' *appearance* of text works such as *Any Moment*, *All Criteria* and

19. Ibid., p. 254.

20. Victor Burgin, 'In Reply', *Art-Language*, vol. 2, no. 2, p. 32; extracted in the Documents section of Osborne, op. cit., p. 238.

21. 'Rules of Thumb', p. 248.

22. 'In Reply', p. 32/238.

IV 2, on the one hand, and the pictorialism of the photo-works, on the other. Yet even in those text works in which Burgin explores the internal conceptual dynamics of logico-linguistic forms of classification, the reader/viewer is always interpellated in the phenomenological space-time of the act of reading. He/she is always addressed directly as 'you'. The communicational dimension is insistent throughout. Correspondingly, even the most pictorial of the photo-works from the late 1970s – such as *Zoo* (1978) – contain elements that direct the viewer towards reflection upon conceptual aspects of their perceptual experience. What changes with the shift in emphasis from 'context' to 'use' is not the conceptual character of the perceptual object but the scope of the context itself. The context is no longer the physical space of the gallery or site, the institutional site of display. Henceforth it will be sign-use within society at large. As Burgin put it in his reply to Art & Language:

Zoo 78
1978–79, one of eight diptychs,
each panel 50 x 75 cm.

> *The optimum function of art … is to modify institutionalised patterns of orientation towards the world and thus to serve as an agency of socialisation. (No art activity therefore is to be understood apart from the codes and practices of the society which contains it; art in use is bracketed ineluctably within ideology.) … we must accept the responsibility of producing art that has more than just Art as its content …*[23]

The most general term governing such practices is 'politics'. By the mid-1970s Burgin's project had become 'the consolidation of conceptualist practices along . . . socialist lines'.[24] The 'break' that occurs in his work around 1973 is thus not a change in the conceptual character of his art, but a radical expansion of its social horizon. This involved a concomitant change in the resources required to theorise it: from phenomenological and analytical philosophies of perception and language to semiotics and ideology-critique.

23. Ibid., p. 34/238.

24. Victor Burgin, 'Socialist Formalism', *Studio International*, vol. 191, no. 980, March/April 1976, p. 148; extracted in the Documents section of Osborne, op. cit., p. 256.

25. 'Rules of Thumb', p. 254.

More than just 'art'

It is an irony of Burgin's development that having rejected Kosuth's analytical model of artistic meaning, on the grounds of the inherently equivocal character of art,[25] he should exchange his own philosophical interest in perception for a competing general theory of meaning, based on a different model of language from Kosuth's: Saussure's semiology, with its basis in general linguistics. In terms of the

73

theoretical resources informing his art, Burgin's definitive distancing of himself from analytical conceptual art thus actually brought him closer to the 'purely conceptual' character of Kosuth's conception of the experience of the artwork.

Burgin's 'Photographic Practice and Art Theory' (1975) might be called 'Art After Semiotics' – except that 'art' has largely disappeared as an articulating concept, to be replaced by the relationship between photography and text.

One thing conceptual art has done, apart from to underline the central importance of theory, is to make the photograph an important tool of practice. The consequence of such moves has been to further render the categorical distinction between art and photography ill-founded and irrelevant.[26]

Yet the fact that photography is as legitimate an artistic means as any other, and of particular importance in engaging the dominant representational codes and in combating the fetishism of the artistic act, does not do away with the question of the specificity of art as a social practice. Henceforth, however, Burgin's writings were to concentrate on 'theories of representation in general', and semiotics and psychoanalysis, in particular. It is within the terms of these theories that his art has largely been received. Yet it is important to distinguish the role of theory as artistic material or productive resource *within* art practice from its more strictly critical, meta-artistic role – however complicated the relationship between the two may be in any particular instance. Indeed, it was precisely this distinction, as manifest in the essentially 'equivocal' status of art (as opposed to the norms of clarity and consistency governing theory), that Burgin deployed against Kosuth: 'The paradoxical nettle always to be grasped is that of reconciling the art work's status as an empty structure with its existence as an assembly of *meaningful* signs.'[27]

Summarising the character of his art of the late 1970s and early 1980s in his book *Between* (1986), Burgin writes of basing his work 'in contemporary cultural theory, rather than in traditional aesthetics'. But this formulation forecloses the middle ground of an anti-aestheticist art theory that was marked out by conceptual art, including Burgin's own early work and writings – ground on which, I would argue, Burgin's art practice continues to rest. In this respect, the retrospectively formulated thesis of the 'end of art theory' conflates the theoretical consequences of the broadening of the social horizon of Burgin's art with its ontological ground

26. Victor Burgin, 'Photographic Practice and Art Theory', *Studio International*, vol. 190, no. 976, July/August 1975, p. 39.

27. 'Rules of Thumb', p. 254.

as a 'message' that depends upon, but is irreducible to, the 'empty structure' of its sensuous form.[28] This difference bears on the question of the 'location' of the work.

In *Between*, Burgin attributes the 'uncertain' location of his work to its cultural-theoretical (rather than aesthetic) ground and he describes it as existing 'between gallery and book; between "visual art" and "theory"; between "image" and "narrative" – "work" providing work between reader and text'.[29] Yet, surely this uncertain location is, more fundamentally, a consequence of the conceptual character of the art – of the distribution of each work *across* (rather than 'between') an infinite yet nonetheless conceptually defined totality of possible realisations or spatio-temporal sites of instantiation. In this specific sense, one might say, a work of conceptual art will be *everywhere, or not at all*.[30] It is this paradoxical de-locatedness, combined with the specific locatedness of each instance of its realisation, that constitutes the affinity of conceptual art with photographic form. In his most recent video and digitally-based photographic work, Burgin continues to exploit the paradoxical spatiality of such art, exploring now its temporalising dimensions, 'consolidating conceptualist practices' with the latest technological forms.

28. Victor Burgin, *Between*, Oxford:Blackwell, 1986, p. 6; 'The End of Art Theory', in Victor Burgin, *The End of Art Theory: Criticism and Postmodernity*, Basingstoke: Macmillan, 1986, pp. 140–204.

29. Victor Burgin, *Between*, Oxford: Blackwell, 1986, p. 6.

30. Cf. Burgin, *In/Different Spaces*, Berkeley and Los Angeles: University of California Press, 1996, p. 31, which cites Lefebvre's *détournement* of Breton's 'Beauty will be compulsive, or it will not be at all': 'Man must be everyday, or he will not be at all.'

Love Letters video projection, 1997

Richard Strauss
Der Rosenkavalier
Act III (fragment), Elisabeth Schwarzkopf

I am compelled to confess to you that I
have not been able to maintain the cool
detachment of the analyst with regard to
Frau G.'s daughter. I can no longer
pretend that what I feel for Elma is
simply the benevolence of the physician
or of a fatherly friend. Frau G. has been
told everything, and my situation is made
both easier and more difficult by her
incomparably kind and loving
attitude toward me.

It is not always easy for the doctor to keep within the limits prescribed by ethics and technique. Those who are still youngish may in particular find it a hard task. Sexual love is undoubtedly one of the chief things in life, and the union of mental and bodily satisfaction in the enjoyment of love is one of its culminating peaks. When a woman sues for love, to reject and refuse is a distressing part for a man to play – for there is an incomparable fascination in a woman of high principles who confesses her passion.

Nietzsche's Paris video projection, 1999–2000

George Frideric Handel

Alcina

Act II Scene VIII

Aria: 'Ah! Mio Cor!' (fragment), Arleen Augér

Da erblickte ich nämlich eine angenehme Arbeitsstube voller Bücher und Blumen,
flankiert von zwei Schlafstuben und – bei uns hin und her gehend – Arbeitskameraden,
zu heiterem und ernstem Kreis geschlossen.

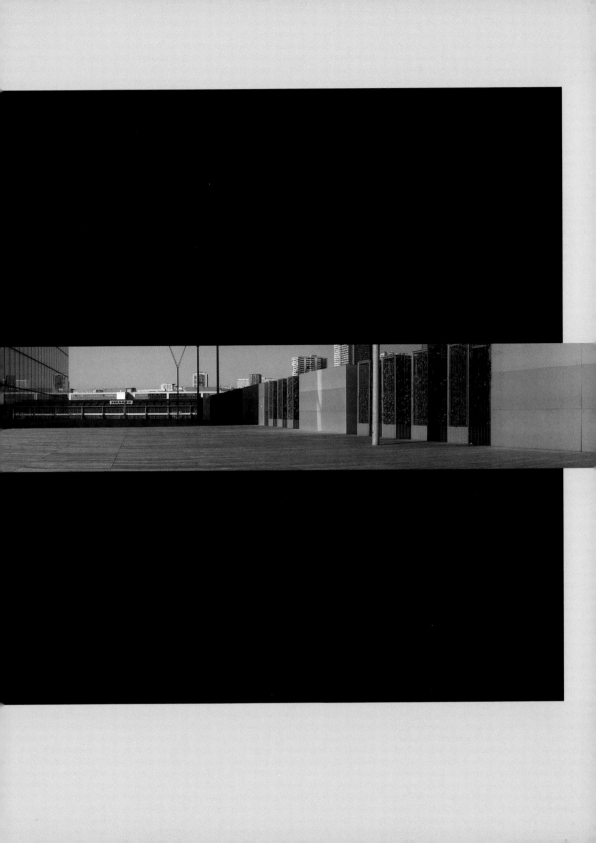

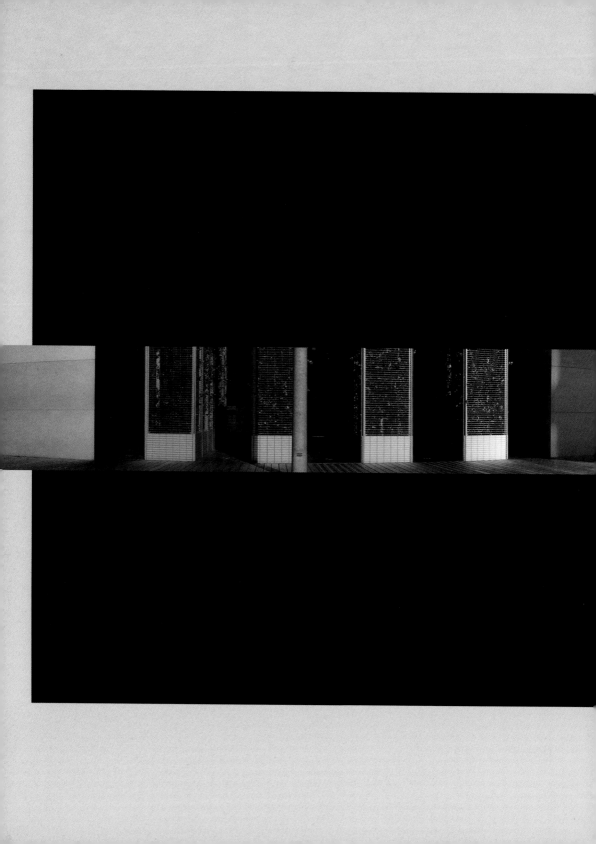

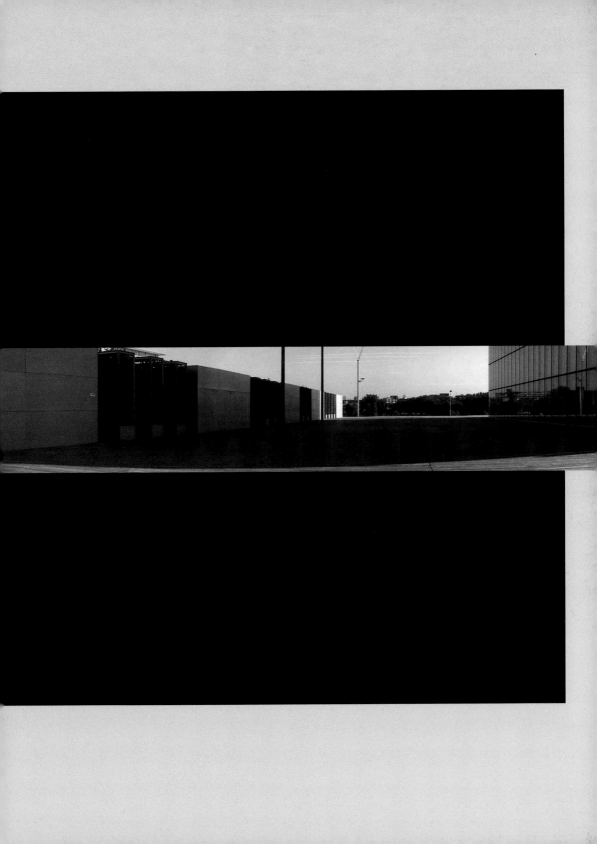

George Frideric Handel

Ariodante

Act II Scene III

Aria: 'Scherza Infida In Grembo Al Drudo' (fragment), Anne Sofie von Otter

I saw a pleasant workroom filled with books and flowers

between   two   bedrooms

Immobile movement
and the speeds of emotion

Françoise Parfait

Nothing is so completely past as a past emotion. Like a person who is a stranger to us, we can only know it in the form of its appearances.
Lou von Salomé [1]

In the vertiginous circle of the eternal return the image dies immediately.
Dino Campana [2]

1. Friederich Nietzsche – Paul Rée – Lou von Salomé, *Correspondance*, Paris: Presses Universitaires de France, 1979, p. 164.

2. Dino Campana, *Opere e Contributi*, vol. 2, Florence: Vallecchi, 1973, p. 1. Quoted by Giorgio Agamben, 'L'image immémoriale', in *Image et mémoire*, Paris: Hoebeke, 1998, p. 77.

My most recent encounter with the work of Victor Burgin was the occasion of a singular emotion. The work in question is *Nietzsche's Paris*, a videographic piece presented at the gallery Durand-Dessert in Paris during the spring of 2001. The emotion in some way 'took me' by surprise, for in this rather abstract work nothing apparent announces itself on the side of pathos; the feeling emerged and developed in the course of my 'observation' of the video projection, without my being able to identify its origin or its cause. Today, I still do not know how much the sentiment owed to my own artistic history or my own intimate experiences, to my diffuse memories or to the art object itself. It is this confusion, nevertheless frequent in the aesthetic relation, which appeared to me at this time as *content* in the very project of Victor Burgin – a project of which one already knows the interest, even obsession, with the mechanisms of memory, allusion, and the vicissitudes of association; with the images and sounds which call us and call up memories, whether individual or collective. In the sphere of criticism and artistic commentary it is not too acceptable to give account of one's emotions in the face of works (for pathos is always suspected of subjectivism), above all when it is a question of proposing an analysis and 'letting the work speak' (rationality so often being credited with objectivity). Nevertheless, it seems to me that the very fact that emotions occur, and are involuntary, is sufficient reason to take them as the basis for an attempt to approach what is at play in the disturbance that the spectator feels – a discreet but tenacious feeling – when confronting the universe that Victor Burgin constructs in his work, whether in this particular work or in others.

The affective point of view

Nietzsche's Paris is a video loop of nine minutes duration, projected on a screen wall. Three types of images make up the sequence. A series of panoramas, filmed from the esplanade of the Bibliothèque Nationale de France, from four different points of view, shows Dominique Perrault's building, its immediate environment, and the city in the distance. Very quickly, the strangeness of these images becomes apparent: there is not a single trace of a living body or a moving object in them; in black and white, everything is frozen. Could this be a video panorama made from a panoramic photograph? Between the panoramas – which are punctuated by a soundtrack that, between very marked silences, allows us to hear fragments from Handel's *Alcina* and *Ariodante* – another image appears in a form opposed in every respect to the panoramas: a static shot, in colour, showing a woman in dark nineteenth-century dress, sitting on a bench in a bower of foliage that trembles in a light breeze, her distant look directed towards the camera. The remaining images are of text, where one can read in a fractional manner: *I saw . . . a pleasant workroom . . . filled with . . . books and flowers . . . between . . . two . . . bedrooms.* Each line of text appears and disappears in a dissolve to the rhythm of the music. In another section of the video one also hears a voice speaking in German: *Da erblickte ich nämlich eine angenehme Arbeitsstube voller Bücher und Blumen, flankiert von zwei Schlafstuben und – bei uns hin und her gehend – Arbeitskameraden, zu heiterem und ernstem Kreis geschlossen.* This enigmatic text gives essentially the same information as the words on the screen, but it also gives voice to a writing and a personality, a fiction embedded in these shots of a Paris petrified under the fascinating gaze of a panoptical Medusa.

Some conditions of rememoration 'in real time' are thus reunited, in the spacing between different registers of images, and in the use of music to impel thought. The panoramas made inside this architecture recall, for example, the ghost – the unconscious? – of the famous *Plan Voisin* that Le Corbusier imagined in 1925, a megalomaniac project of terrifying beauty which consisted of razing Paris to erect monumental city-towers. The panoramas give the modern city – of which one glimpses the different layers of its heterogeneous construction – a frozen and unliveable image in which the body is caught in the trap of its central position, with no possibility of changing places with that which it sees – like the wind-break bushes on the esplanade, held in the vice-like grip of grilled cages. Further, the relation between movement and immobility confers a quite indefinable status on the image: *What is this?* is the big question that language poses to objects and images. In fact, Burgin has transformed a filmed sequence into still images, has modified them, then reanimated them – digitally – to produce the panoramic movement. The shot of the woman from another *époque* consoles the spectator of this synthetic urban vision that gives no real look, for in spite of its fixity this image expresses the tremor of the living.

There is nothing here of melancholy or resentment (for it is nonetheless a question of Nietzsche – the title of the piece alerts the visitor to this). This is not some monument erected to the philosopher of modernity, but a homage to a love story – involving Lou von Salomé, Friedrich Nietzsche, and their mutual friend Paul Rée – as fleeting as it was dazzling, which for a time nourished plans for a *ménage-à-trois* in Paris. The project was never realised and love was betrayed, but Lou von Salomé united the trio in a dream which she recounted as reproduced on the soundtrack. A panel of text situated at the entrance to the room informs the visitor of this historical episode, allowing them to place Lou's recollection – read and heard in the video – in context. It is nevertheless not necessary to know the story in order to profit from Victor Burgin's *aesthetic* proposition (in which affect and modernity confront each other), to arrive at that state of availability of mind which allows the organisation of sensations into a mental construct where one's own baggage, affective and conceptual, nourishes the perception of the work. In effect, it is mainly because of the very movement of the video, its rhythms and durations, that emotion is born and thickens. Etymologically, 'emotion' is a putting in motion (*ex-movere* – to put in movement) which describes a sensation, agreeable or disagreeable, considered from an affective point of view. Emotion is here inscribed in the unfurling of images and sounds, in the song which carries the voice for the time of an expiration, of a breath which regenerates itself in the silences, in the frames which suspend movement in order to better perceive a trembling, or seem to introduce movement inside a still life. Such movement is perceptible in the body, in the very flesh of the spectator – it is so true that it can even give 'goosebumps'. But it also brings with it a more profound and buried movement – that which searches memory for analogous sensations, for memories made available by the actualisation of their effects on perception. This is something very difficult to describe for one does not objectively know to what it corresponds, whether it concerns only one's own history or whether the intimacy of the sensation touches a common experience.

Remembering, Repeating 1995, two-screen video projection

3. To exercise this faculty of the brain (memory), one must, according to the advice of Simonides, 'select distinct sites in thought, form images of things that one wishes to retain, then arrange these images on the various sites. Thus the order of places conserves the order of things; the images recall the things themselves. The places are the tablets of wax upon which one writes; the images are the letters that one traces there.' Cicero, *De l'orateur*, 11–LXXXVI–352.354, Paris: Les Belles Lettres, 1966, pp. 153–54.

Panorama and the travelling shot as movements of memory

If memory inscribes itself in places, as Simonides proposes,[3] and if images recall the things themselves, then Burgin's videos are an invitation to travel in the space of memory – not so much a particular memory, a singular object which focuses imaginative attention upon itself, but *memory* in general. Beyond the use of archive images which constitute veritable switching mechanisms for collective memory (for example, the black-and-white image of the silhouette of a woman in *Love Letters* – an anonymous passer-by filmed by the Princess Bonaparte in the streets of Vienna in 1939 – or the citations of images from *Vertigo* and *Pépé le Moko* in the video *Venise* and the installation *Remembering, Repeating*), and beyond the literary and cinematographic references having to do with memory and the psychical apparatus

– very numerous and very precise in Burgin's work – the treatment of movement, and of speeds of movement, tends to create a *tempo* which is that of rememoration (as the title of *Remembering, Repeating* clearly indicates). The panorama and the travelling shot constitute a first group of image movements that allow the mnemic work to be set in motion; the second group plays upon the internal temporal relations between movement and fixity of the image.

The four panoramas of *Nietzsche's Paris*, as already noted, are filmed from four different points of view on the esplanade of the Bibliothèque Nationale de France. Each of the points of view corresponds to the mid-point of the four sides of the rectangle that forms the area. The panoramas taken from the long sides are repeated twice while those taken from the short sides make only a single revolution. The images obtained in this way are closely similar in appearance (the uniformity of the architecture contributes to this), similar in nature (the movement of all the panoramas is perfectly regular), but not identical. The spectator has trouble in deciding precisely in what way they are not identical, and this indecision, this recognition of the inadequacy of perception, obliges them to search on the side of older and more memorable impressions. This approach is in a movement which tries to *go towards*, but also in the fixity of the point of view that all panoramas imply and which makes of them a form both enclosed and closed upon itself. The body which bears the look is assigned a central place, that of the watcher in the Benthamite tradition of panopticism. In slightly displacing the point of view for each panorama Burgin allows some 'play', relieves the tension induced by an axis of vision fixed on a single point and thus allows the imaginary to circulate in the interstices opened between the two rotating movements. A light vertigo emanates from these displacements which lead from the circle to the spiral. As Raymond Bellour has noted in his reflection on the self portrait: 'The road that leads from memory to invention is circular; the circles repeat themselves and inscribe themselves one inside the other without ever coinciding, in a progression which is not a progress, but a controlled drifting'.[4] Thus, this interval between one movement and another, in provoking a mental movement, allows a shifting in memory between regions, sediments, layers – all the topography of memory that Gilles Deleuze defined in the 1980s. It may also recall the Eternal Return dear to Nietzsche, a return not of the same but of the similar, in which is configured the movement of a desire ceaselessly renewed.

4. Raymond Bellour, *L'Entre-Images, Photo, Cinéma, Vidéo*, Paris: La Différence, 1990, p. 309.

The other image movement that Burgin uses as a metaphor for the interior journey is the travelling shot: a forward travelling in *Venise*, a lateral travelling in *Love Letters*, for example. The travelling shot – this cinematographic form inherited from the painted panoramas of the nineteenth century, and the first journeys by train – proposes a manner of traversing the world according to a configuration of the visible determined by the optics and the shutter speed of cameras. Before being recorded by cameras, the 'travelling' had provided the traveller with a new visual experience which modified his perception of the depth of the visual field: according to the speed of the train, the immediate foreground is blurred, the plane of focus beyond demands an effort of accommodation, the plane beyond that corresponds to the essential of the field of vision, and the distant background seems almost fixed at infinity. The traveller's gaze is thus submitted to a real work of adaptation, accentuated by their lateral movement which commits them to a perturbing coming and going; this is why the look has a tendency to fix itself on a plane parallel to the track and to focus itself upon this plane. Cameras reproduce more or less the same model, and must be adjusted in relation to a choice of focal plane.

In *Love Letters*, the image shot from the train travelling between Budapest and Vienna (the voyage as mental experience; the travelling shot as a form of representation likely to encourage or provoke a similar experience in the immobile spectator; the *road movie* as genre) allows the glass of the window, sprinkled with raindrops, to appear sharply in focus: the raindrops serve to materialise the foreground and therefore to establish a relationship between the look situated in the interior, in the sphere of intimacy, and the landscape which appears, as a technical consequence, relatively out of focus. This aspect of the image does not simply create a succession in depth of field of more or less sharp planes, and of variable speeds of movement between these planes; to these spatial considerations are added temporal considerations which make for all the interest of this travelling shot. The foreground with its very sharp drops of water, very close, is the image of the present (close to the look, indicating the state of the weather: it is raining, here and now), while the out-of-focus background, in which various planes of the landscape pass at different speeds into the distance, is a representation of time, if not past, at least in the process of becoming past. To take an expression from Paul Virilio, depth of field and 'depth

Love Letters
1997, three-screen video projection

of time' are conjugated and confused together: the more distant the planes are from the foreground, the slower are the speeds of their unfurling; the further away they are, the less they move. So it is with memory – the older the memory is, the more it is fixed in an immobile schematic representation, the more difficult it is to resurrect it and make it present.

An immobile movement

Beyond the use of real movement in and of the image, Burgin foregrounds the internal temporal relations between the movement of the image and its fixity, its suspension, its arrest upon itself (as one says, 'arrested motion'); he interrogates the permeable frontiers between the photographic and the cine- or videographic. The window and its drops of water in the foreground are the photographic part of this travelling shot; he reminds us, along with Roland Barthes, that 'photography belongs to that class of laminated objects of which one cannot separate the two layers without destroying them: the window and the landscape, and why not: Good and Evil, desire and its object: dualities which one can conceive, but not perceive'.[5] The window is like a screen which makes visible and which covers at the same time: fixed image and fixed idea, desire and its object. An analogy with the psycho-analytic model might be seen in this form which shows in an image the different levels of consciousness of memory, even the 'screen memory' materialised by the window glass in the foreground. And then there is the suspension of movement in the real arrested motion; the journey is interrupted for an instant, the flow of time is prevented, the arrow of time and of duration become contradictory. The freezing of movement opens a breach in the perception of a continuous time and the gap in the mental representation of this perception. If 'to perceive means to immobilise' as Bergson says in *Matter and Memory*,[6] in condensing very long periods of time into a few differentiated moments, then a veritable effort of perception is required of us by the panoramas of *Nietzsche's Paris*, in which there is a hiatus between the time deployed in the course of the panoramas and the time without duration (or iconic content) of these same panoramas. The image that the panoramas unfold is one in which there is no subjective duration: in black and white, without a living soul, which might be understandable given the inhospitability of the place, but even more so when one is more attentive. From the traffic to the smoke escaping from the industrial chimneys of Paris and its inner suburbs, from the cranes and building sites neighbouring the trees on the opposite bank of the river, nothing moves, as if enchanted, and yet objectively it endures, because the inexorable

5. Roland Barthes, *La chambre claire*, Paris: Gallimard, 1980, p. 17.

6. Henri Bergson, *Matière et Mémoire*, Paris: puf, 1993, p. 233.

panorama unrolls all this within its frame. Photographic time, which is to say instantaneity, the fraction of the second seized by the camera, is dilated into a cinematic temporality, the time proper to film and to its technical possibilities, and so creates a representation of what one might call a 'dead time'.[7] Space is represented without duration, or in a duration with neither beginning nor end, a duration without event: otherwise expressed, a non duration. One thinks of *La Région Centrale*, a film made by Michael Snow in 1970 with the aid of a camera controlled by a computer that he had installed in the north of Canada in a rocky and deserted region. The images taken by the camera attached to an articulated arm formed panoramas realised in all directions and according to very different speeds, orientations and rhythms. These images without any regard, recorded by a surveillance apparatus and not by a living and desiring body, seem to recall a prehuman state of the world, without either language or drama. The panoramas of *Nietzsche's Paris* and those of *La Région Centrale* resemble each other in a certain manner in that they deploy a 'space less here' and a 'time less now', to adopt the formulations of Thierry de Duve.[8] These images are 'paradoxical', like the sleep of the same name during which the dreamer produces rapid eye movements: the here and now of the image is collapsed into the fixed colour shot of this woman who poses while looking at us from within a fragment of shivering nature. It is really in this suspension of the image – whether of its own time or of its own movement (and we shall see that these are not the same thing) – that the perception is constructed and the mental impulse released which will inaugurate the search for one's own emotions in memory.

7. I refer here to the work by Emmanuel Carlier called *Temps Mort*; it consists of projecting one after another, like a film, photographs made at the same moment by some fifty cameras arranged in a circle around a subject in movement.

8. Thierry de Duve, 'Michael Snow. Les déictiques de l'expérience, et au-delà', in *Les Cahiers du Musée Nationale d'Art Moderne*, no. 50, winter 1994.

Vertigo, the fall and the Eternal Return

The analogical image, whether it be photographic, cine- or videographic, always constitutes more or less a return: return to that which has been and return to the places where that took place. If this last is possible because it is always possible to return to one's home country (spaces change but do not disappear), it is not the same for time, which bears the mark of irreversibility. It is this impossibility of the return of time which can produce a nostalgia that can at times tend towards a melancholic attitude: when Burgin shows in several works (for example, *Lichtung*, *Another Case History*) the silhouette of a woman seen from behind, immobile or disappearing into a wood, he cites,

Left: *Lichtung*, 1998-99, single-screen video projection
Right: *Another Case History*, 1999, single-screen video projection

certainly, the Madeleine of Hitchcock's *Vertigo*, but equally he puts in place the melancholic figure of an impossible turning back, the impossible reversibility of presence. The cinema, and later video, very quickly explored and exploited the possibility they possessed, thanks to their technical or technological apparatus, to artificially break this irreversibility of time by reverse motion – which had astounded the first spectators of the cinematograph – or by the use of the loop, inscribed in the very unreeling of the film strip, or in the form of the repetition made possible and widespread thanks to the tape recorder. So if the panorama

figures the return, in the successive unrolling of similar shots representing a space without duration, the repetition of an archival image or a cinematic shot showing the movement of a body, will also constitute a form of return: return of the gesture and with it the return of film, which is to say of the imaginary that it deploys, and return there again of the memory of the

Venise
1993, video, 30 minutes

spectator. Burgin often uses this form of repetition: certainly one of the models which seems to haunt him is Hitchcock's *Vertigo* which presents at one and the same time forms of repetition in the tale (with the use of ghosts and doubles) and in the story which is made of it (return to places, similarity of shots). The repetition of the fall is striking for, beyond a scenic necessity, its reiteration gives it an emblematic value of crime and redemption, abandonment and reparation. Here vertigo anticipates the fall, and is equally the consequence of it.

It is in his installation *Remembering, Repeating* that Burgin very clearly uses the fall as return in time. He seems to reply to the question put by Laurent Jenny: 'The fall interrogates time, which slips away; would we have fallen without this *lapsus* of an instant which has not been lived, which cannot be refound?'[9] The false step and the fall of *Pépé le Moko* in Duvivier's film are those of a man vanquished by nostalgia for Paris, and by his frantic and lost love; his stumbling anticipates his definitive fall into death and marks the impossible return to France, to Paris and childhood. The repetition, doubled by an effect of slow-motion, makes this plan the emblem of emotion for 'to feel is to fall, to allow oneself to sink under what just happens to us'[10] in order afterwards to be able to redispose oneself in the world. As he often does in his citations of films or archive shots, Burgin 'unsticks' the sequence by Duvivier by changing its medium (from film to video), by slowing it down (or in more generally changing its speed and its rhythm), and by repeating

9. Laurent Jenny, *L'expérience de la chute*, Paris: puf, 1997, p. 13.

10. Ibid., p. 14.

it as a loop or inserting it between images of a different nature. The *lapsus* that Jenny speaks of becomes recognised as a symptom when one sees, on the screen facing the one on which Jean Gabin stumbles, an anonymous and multiracial crowd filing by on the moving walkway of a Parisian metro. Burgin shot these scenes in 1995 at the Montparnasse metro station, a site of Islamicist terrorist attacks that same year. French colonial history is inscribed in the diversity of geographical origins of the people who pass on the moving walkway, people with passive and inward-looking faces. These passers-by take on the value of signifiers of the colonisation evoked in *Pépé le Moko*; they allow us to reflect and to project upon them the fiction on the facing screen, and the mnemic and reflexive process is again set in motion. From the stumbling of a fictional hero to the stumbling of the history of peoples, the link is established in the *face à face* and in the slowed and tenacious repetition actualised in the documentary images. Here cinema constitutes the memory of a history that video reworks to make readable. This representation consists of the return of the absent or repressed into the here and now.

Video, amnesia and disappearance

Burgin's videographic work rests on the qualities of the medium and inscribes itself in a history of evanescent images. In recycling cinema images, in treating them with the digital possibilities of electronic means, in managing silences or in using music as breath and counterpoint to the images, in punctuating the soundtrack and the unfurling of images with sounds, words, texts related to psychoanalysis and its actors, Burgin is one of the important artists who have exploited psychical processes and the fabrication of memories with the techniques of the time-image, the mobile image. Along with Thierry Kuntzel, Gary Hill, Bill Viola occasionally, Stan Douglas, but also Chris Marker or Atom Egoyan and many others, Victor Burgin's installations participate in a veritable elaboration of a thinking of amnesia with videographic tools; they also participate in the elaboration of a videographic aesthetic now spreading into practices of all kinds, whatever their media. Video, this technology 'between' the cinema and the computer, from a historical and technical point of view, has constituted a fragile and sensitive parenthesis between these two registers of images. Between the image and the absence of the image video is also situated between the analogical and the numerical, between object and process, between visible and invisible, between the direct and the deferred, between the mobile and the immobile, between outside and inside, between above and below, between sleep and waking . . . between appearance and disappearance. If video is so apt at treating disappearance, it is because it is itself – structurally, technically and historically – inhabited by disappearance and in process of disappearing as a specific medium. It is its evanescent character, its evanescent ontology, which inscribes the videographic between disappearance and fading; that is to say, between appearance as trace of an absent object, which nevertheless exists but which is hidden from view, and the appearance of this object as being in the process of fading, of losing consciousness, or disappearing from consciousness and of becoming phantom. Videographic bodies are seized by spectrality – as Derrida puts it, their traces are the present of their absence. This is because video is founded upon a deficit of analogical representation, because its conservation is aleatory and unstable, because it is by constitution temporal, and because it is itself a model of loss. In the image of memory, it is inhabited by disappearance and forgetting – what it brings to light are the already ruined forms of a visibility always incomplete, often menaced, sometimes impossible. Video doubtless cannot give account of loss in figurative form – is such a figure conceivable? – but it can deploy the processes of loss and of disappearance, seize the operations at play in the process of effacement.

If video has never ceased to work and be worked by disappearance, it is because the epoch in which it appeared had nothing but this historical and anthropological urgency to confront. Video has constituted a tool particularly adapted to elaborate new formulations of our relationship with an increasingly elusive, rapid and uncontrollable world, crushed by the weight of a memory whose reference points are increasingly difficult to make out.

At a time when programmatic ideologies of the effacement of history take on new vigour in the cultures of the personified image, Burgin's work again grasps the fragility of sensation, the complexity of memory and the condition of forgetting. He does not hesitate to use the tools of information technology to – point by point, on the surface of the image, of the screen, of the present – pursue his exploration of reminiscence and of the recall of memory. Of the deflagration of transience and the need to remember it.

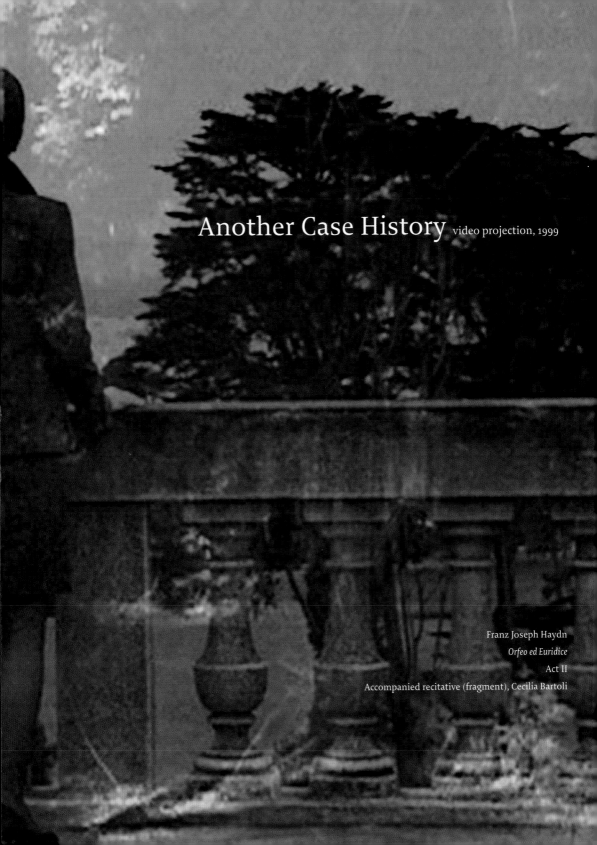

Another Case History video projection, 1999

Franz Joseph Haydn
Orfeo ed Euridice
Act II
Accompanied recitative (fragment), Cecilia Bartoli

Her eyelids trembled open   He took her hand   'You're not dead,' he said

He pressed her fingers to his lips   'Never look back,' he said

Silently   Violently   The waters break   Around the emerging form

Of a woman   Her tanned flanks   Streaming water   She folds a towel

Around her new-born body   Long shadows of palms   Lie   Across the pool

Falling   Upon the glass walls   Of the corridor   Where he takes his last case

From the room   And closes the door

Elective Affinities video installation, 2000–2001

Anonymous, seventeenth century
'En esta larga ausencia', Victoria de los Ángeles

Many years have passed
since he left for the war.
Although the war is long over
there has been no news of him.
Other men now press her to marry.

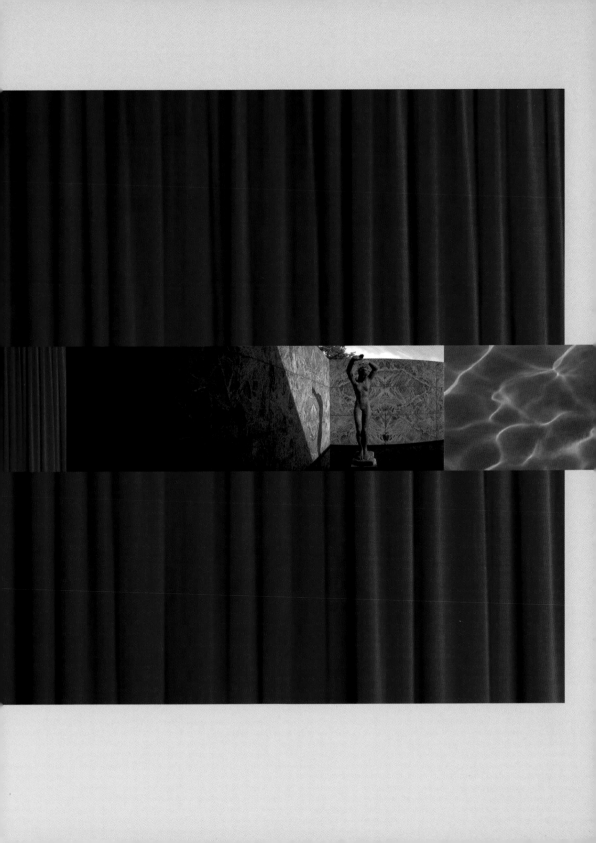

She says she will choose between them
when she has finished her weaving.
She weaves all day.
At night she unravels her work.
Next day she begins again.

Where to begin?

Victor Burgin

Everyone who had been out for an evening stroll was gone.

W.G. Sebald, *The Rings of Saturn*

The England to which I returned after 'September 11' felt itself under siege for the first time in sixty years, with the difference that no one could now say to what extent the threat was real. Invited to make a new work for Arnolfini in Bristol, a city one approaches by train from London through some of the most pleasant countryside in England, I recalled *Listen to Britain*, a film which opens with a similarly pastoral scene. The twenty-minute black-and-white short, directed by Humphrey Jennings and edited by Stewart McAllister, was produced by the Crown Film Unit in 1942 when Britain seemed imminently at risk of invasion. What most intrigues me about *Listen to Britain* is that, at a time of extreme national danger, it neither exhorts nor prognosticates; it contains neither commentary nor dialogue, and neither shows nor names the enemy. Jennings' picture of a nation at war displaces conflict beyond the edge of the frame; the threat of violence is everywhere but itself appears nowhere. This characteristic of the film seemed peculiarly apposite to the state of the nation to which I had returned. My recollection of this short film in turn led me to think of a short sequence from another film made two years later, in 1944, which again exiles war beyond the borders of an essentially rural idyll. The sequence is from Michael Powell and Emeric Pressburger's *A Canterbury Tale*. A young woman in a light summer dress climbs a path onto the Downs above Canterbury. Emerging from a stand of trees she is suddenly confronted with a view of the cathedral. The screen frames her entranced face in close-up as she hears ancient sounds on the wind: jingling harnesses, pipes and lutes. She turns her head swiftly left and right, as if looking for the source of the sounds – which abruptly stop as the close-up cuts to a long-shot of her alone and small in the bright expanse of grassland. The young woman on the Downs experiences the abrupt and unexpected return of an image from a common history, and hears sounds from a shared past that haunts the hill. Powell and Pressburger's film ends with the sound of organ music in Canterbury Cathedral. Jennings' film ends with the sound of a virtuoso piano recital in London's National Gallery.

A half-century later, the London Symphony Orchestra is putting an artwork in a concert venue. The LSO is making a home for its *Discovery* programme in St Luke's, an early eighteenth-century church on Old Street in London's East End. A commission for an artist is included in the redevelopment plan. The brief states: 'the commissioned Work will make reference to both the impressive architecture of the building, and its role as a music and education venue. The recommended site is the architecturally impressive stair lobby at the entrance to the building.'

Staircases were favoured places for the *trompe-l'œil* extension of real space into fictive space that often complements Baroque architecture. By the time St Luke's was built, about fifty such painted staircases had been executed in London houses and country mansions. These decorations might have an allegorical or mythical content alluding to the use of the building and the identity of its owner. For St Luke's, the Orpheus myth imposes itself as all but inevitable. The myth anticipates a founding doctrine (the Resurrection) of the religion the building once celebrated (Christian exegesis of the Orpheus myth dates from about AD 200). After being derelict for over forty years the building itself is now being brought back to life. Most importantly, the Orpheus myth is a hymn to the power of music that, since its origins in Classical antiquity, has survived in countless retellings to the present day. The trajectory of Baroque opera may be traced in its terms – from the *L'Orfeo* of Claudio Monteverdi (1607), to the *L'Orfeo ed Euridice* of Christoph Willibald von Gluck (1762). More recent history offers cinematic versions, such as Jean Cocteau's *Orphée* (1949), where death rides in a Rolls Royce, escorted by motorcycle police, and Marcel Camus' *Orfeu Negro* (1959) in which Orpheus is a samba-playing Rio de Janeiro labourer. Orpheus descends into the underworld to bring Eurydice back to the world of the living. Early versions of the myth describe him searching for her among crowds of ghosts. From St Luke's Church it is a short allegorical step to the nearby Old Street station of the crowded London Underground.[1]

The LSO *Discovery* programme's inaugural broadcast was of Benjamin Britten's *The Young Person's Guide to the Orchestra (Variations and Fugue on a Theme of Henry Purcell, Op. 34)*. In music commissioned for a film by the Ministry of Education, Britten cites the work of a Baroque composer. Looking for a formal structure for my video it occurred to me to listen to Britten, and begin where he began – with the eight-measure 'hornpipe' theme from Purcell's incidental music for the play *Abdelazar*. When I went looking for Purcell's score I found that the complete title of the play is *Abdelazar, or The Moor's Revenge*.

1. After writing this note on the LSO work in progress, and nine months into the project, I received news that the local planning authority has withheld consent for the video. An appeal is in process.

Listen to Britain work in progress, 2002

The eye of man hath not heard,
the ear of man hath not seen
A Midsummer Night's Dream

Landscape

Girl crosses frame
walking uphill

Dissolve
to view
downhill

Long-shot
Girl walking towards
camera

Dissolve
to woods
Girl approaching camera

Girl stops
Looks out of frame

Cut
View of distant cathedral

Cut
Close-up of girl
listening all around her

American servicemen
in the village
cannot find
local girls
who will go out with them
At night
the Glue Man
emerges from shadows
pours glue on a girl's hair
then disappears

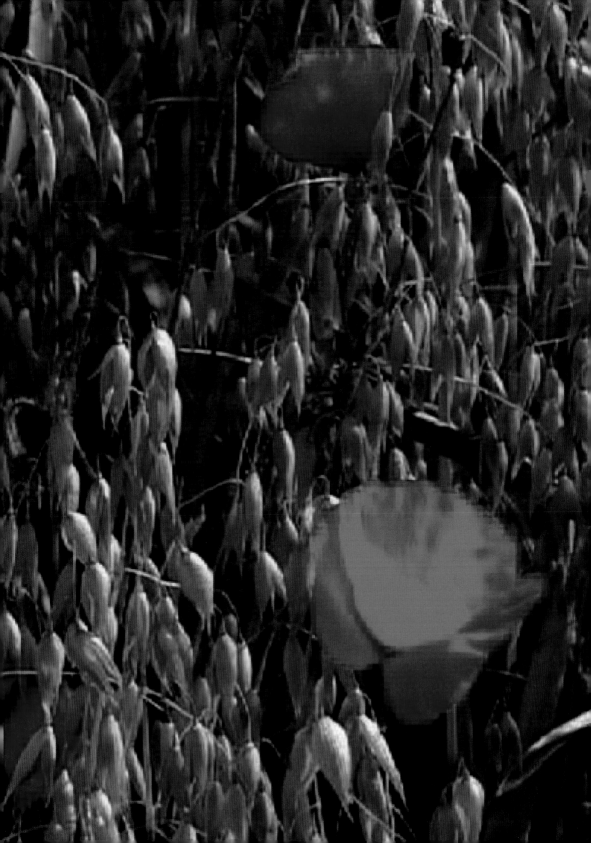

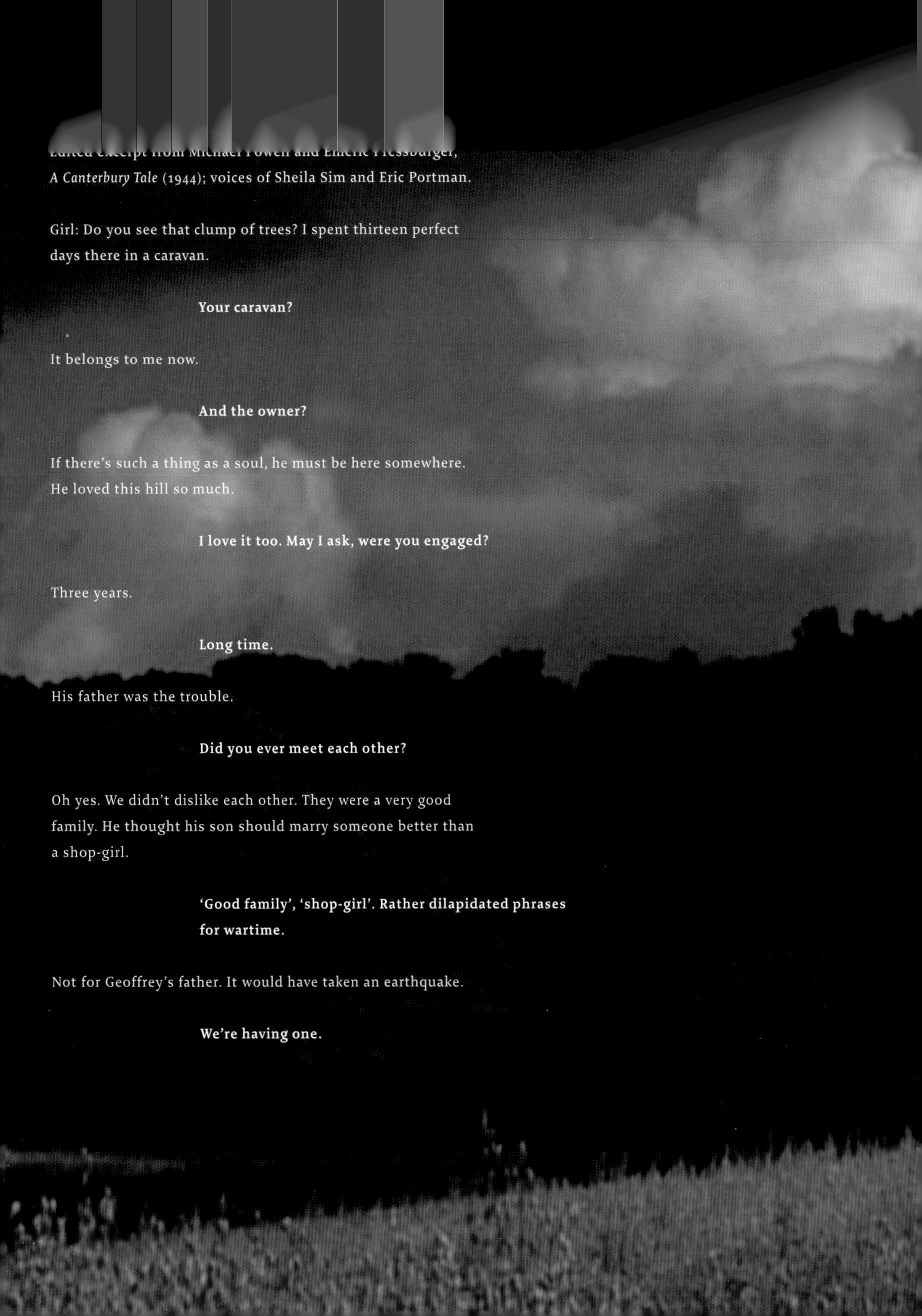

Edited excerpt from Michael Powell and Emeric Pressburger,
A Canterbury Tale (1944); voices of Sheila Sim and Eric Portman.

Girl: Do you see that clump of trees? I spent thirteen perfect
days there in a caravan.

Your caravan?

It belongs to me now.

And the owner?

If there's such a thing as a soul, he must be here somewhere.
He loved this hill so much.

I love it too. May I ask, were you engaged?

Three years.

Long time.

His father was the trouble.

Did you ever meet each other?

Oh yes. We didn't dislike each other. They were a very good
family. He thought his son should marry someone better than
a shop-girl.

**'Good family', 'shop-girl'. Rather dilapidated phrases
for wartime.**

Not for Geoffrey's father. It would have taken an earthquake.

We're having one.

Music: edited excerpt from Benjamin Britten,
A Midsummer Night's Dream (1960); libretto adapted from
Shakespeare by Benjamin Britten and Peter Pears;
voice of Alfred Deller in the role of Oberon.

There sleeps Tytania, sometime of the night,
Lull'd in these flowers, with dances
and delight
[. . .]
And with the juice of this I'll streak her eyes,
And make her full of hateful fantasies.